THE BUTTERFLY CLUB

"Is That You?"

PHYLLIS CALVEY

ISBN: 1501032054

ISBN 13: 9781501032059

Library of Congress Control Number: 2014915736

Createspace Independent Publishing Platform

North Charleston, South Carolina

DEDICATION

To Hailey Brant, who inspired this book

To Caleb Brant, and Ella and Jack Calvey
Our talks about God fill my life with insight and joy!

Acknowledgments

To Michael, "my Conway". I appreciate and am forever grateful for all the time you spent editing this manuscript. You know the ins and outs of this book as much as I do. Your editing was like a magic wand that touched my manuscript with style. (Why can't I put a comma where I would naturally take a breath?) Yet, even more than this, I thank you for your constant support, encouragement, and generosity that continues to overwhelm me. My Conway is a gift from God!

To Steve Baird. Thank you for your kindness in supporting our ministry through the years, and especially for this endeavor. It has made a great difference in our lives and, hopefully, in each life that the book reaches.

To Jessie, my dearest daughter. It was during our endless conversations about the butterfly club that the book took shape, and I was able to find those hidden pieces. It never would have happened without your patience and insight. You were there every step of the way! I was so moved to read the signs God had shared with you. Your writing is disarmingly honest, perfectly capturing what is longed for after a loved one has died. You are such a gifted writer. Thank You!

To Trevor, my dear son. I realize only too well the places in your heart you had to revisit to write about the signs you had experienced, and the precious time you gave to this during the business of your own family's life. As always, your writing is so powerful and unique. And as much as I have come to expect this from you, I was constantly delighted by how you described each situation and emotion. You will touch the hearts of many, and I am so proud of your many talents. Thank you!

To Bob and Linda Dagesse. You were entrusted from above with the seed for The Butterfly Club. And only through your love and faith in God could it be planted. Your daughter AnneMarie's eternal spirit of goodness is giving a name to the shared experience of having had a sign from God. The promise has been kept; you are still in the fight together! I am so blessed you came into my life.

To Jackie Eaton. Thank you so much for sharing your beautiful butterfly stories, and introducing me to the man who first said the words, "Welcome to the butterfly club." There would not be a book without you. You and your sister, Madonna, were indeed the first two official members!

To Jodi O'Grady. Thank you for being there as my personal tech support in the midst of everyone needing your time. Your expertise was greatly appreciated, and your patience and love, invaluable.

To the innumerable people who have experienced the butterfly phenomenon, or a sign from God. Your stories and spirit kept me going. And thank you to all who have shown such an interest in this book. Writing is often very lonely, but you made me feel encouraged and surrounded by the love and support of good friends!

To John Paul, Danny, Ira, Pépè Phil, Carrine, Red and AnneMarie. Thank you for sending us a sign that there is another side!

From Phyllis and Brian,
two who love God joined as one...

Do you have a story to share?

I would love to hear if you have experienced a butter-fly sign or another sign God has chosen to communicate with you.

Also, it would mean so much if you had the time to share which story was your favorite, and how it affected you.

I welcome you to The Butterfly Club and hope you will invite others that we may share with each other these incredible signs of God's presence!

http://www.butterflyclubbook.com/

TABLE OF CONTENTS

HOW GREAT *ARE* HIS SIGNS!

(DANIEL 4:3)

PROLOGUE

M y dearest Hailey, my first-born granddaughter, to finally answer your question. It was December, two weeks before Christmas, and it was freezing. We always seemed to pick the coldest night to go to the

National Shrine of our Lady of LaSalette. This has been our family tradition since your Uncle Trevor and your mom were little, and it was so wonderful that we could continue the tradition with you when you were born.

Our plan never changed; it was imperative we be there before the lights went on. At ten of five you'd find us standing on the top of the stairs where many people made their way up the middle on their knees. Even when you were very young you could anticipate the excitement of seeing the darkness all at once light up with thousands of lights. Hailey, it's the little things that make memories. Like when you always took one piece of golden straw from the life-size Nativity to put in your coat pocket to remind yourself to be especially good until Christmas. How all of us would throw our pennies in the fountain every year, trying so hard to land them exactly where we wanted, as if that would increase the chance to make our prayer come true. The softness on my cheek when you and Caleb would innocently whisper your prayer in my ear. And, of course, your mom always teasing when I had to read every single billboard at each display.

That particular year you were four-and-a-half years old. It was a Friday night and your dad was driving. The van was still freezing when Grandpa took his seat in the front with your dad, I got in the middle seat with Caleb who was two-and-a-half, and you and your mom sat in the way back. We were all snuggled deep into our warm clothes as we made our way up the hill to the main road. Though it was only four o'clock it was already dark. Suddenly Caleb pointed out the window and said, "Look, Grandma, Luna." He and I always called the moon Luna back then, and we even had a song to go with it. Well, I bent down to peer out the window on his side and saw the biggest winter moon I had ever seen. It was so full and round and low in the sky that it brought heaven down to where it seemed we could just reach out and touch it. The heat had finally permeated the van making us all warm and cozy. I will never forget how quiet it was, which was never normal when we were all together, especially if you were there Hailey! And it was more than the silence of not talking. It was the feeling of stillness described in the scriptures when God is about to speak. Out of that stillness you said very softly, "I miss Ira." In that moment all the memories of that sad morning flooded in.

I was with you and your mom that morning when she got the phone call. We both knew something terrible had happened. Your mom never cried, and when you saw her crying you began to cry too. You put your little arm around her, and never let her go during that whole conversation. It was Memaw calling to tell your mom that Ira had died in a car crash early that morning, June 13, 2002. Your mom couldn't accept that it was true. She was waiting for something, anything, to happen to say it had all been a terrible mistake, that he really wasn't dead.

Ira was 32 years old. He had always worked long hours, holidays, and on the weekends too, but that last year everything in his life seemed to be changing. He was going through some difficult times. To make matters worse, he had back surgery and was in constant pain. He stayed for six months at your Memaw's house to recover. At that time Memaw and Pop lived just around the corner from your house. While Ira was staying there you had a chance to get close to him. He'd pick out a special movie for you at least once a week and you'd watch it just the two of you. He showed you his Star Wars collection and old cars and loads of things he loved to collect. He called you his little Pineapple Head. He loved you so much; you were his little pal.

Ira was four years older than your dad and the outgoing one in the family. Ira was the showman, the storyteller, the comedian. He was always the center of attention. On the other hand, your dad was the quiet one. He possessed a quick wit and said his perfect one liners in the background of Ira's stage. When Ira died your dad never spoke of his feelings, never said his name, and didn't really want anyone else to mention it either. It was too difficult, too painful to lose his only brother, his best friend, the leader of all the neighborhood friends, including Uncle Trevor. And so, in the car that night, when you said, "I miss Ira," no one was sure just what to say.

I remember turning to look back at you and saw the tears in your eyes. Your favorite little stuffed animal,

Butterscotch, was with you in your car seat, and you squeezed him close to you. In a small voice that was trying hard not to cry, you said, "Grandma, can God talk to us?"

That was the night you inspired me to write this book. I knew if you could hear the story of the butterfly club as it unfolded from the very beginning, your question would be answered. I promised I would one day tell you about all of these things. And you kept reminding me of that promise until I did! Thank you for never losing interest. It has been a long time coming, but I have no doubt it is all taking place exactly as it was meant to.

Hailey, God communicates with people differently; revealing His presence and speaking to them in personal ways only they can understand. I have felt God speak to me in many ways. Sometimes He speaks words He wants me to hear through another person. When I am preparing to give a presentation for the Lighthouse Ministry, where Grandpa and I teach through story and song, I have learned to hear God's voice through feelings I get when I study and am searching for that perfect story to go with the scripture-based songs Grandpa has written. But my favorite way God communicates with me is through signs. When I saw my very first sign, God felt so close that it literally took my breath away. It was unexpected, surprising, and so wonderful that I wanted more signs. Who wouldn't? But through the years, I've found it never works to ask God for a sign. Signs come to you only in God's perfect timing.

From the time you asked the question, Hailey, I knew I wanted to write this book, and it never left my mind or heart. I was so excited. I wanted to begin right away, and yet, there was a part of me that could not deny that I felt God wanting me to continue with the Lighthouse Ministry for a while longer. This exacted a lot of patience, and it was not going to be an easy decision to make. Grandpa and I had been teaching and traveling together for the last 20 years. He loved our Ministry just the way it was and didn't want it to change. My writing would greatly affect his life as well, at least for a few years. We continued to give our presentations. During all that time, I prayed for God's guidance. And, one year, when our programs ended for the season, I knew without a doubt that God was telling me it was time now to begin, but how would I tell Grandpa?

On a Monday morning when we took our usual walk around the lake before breakfast, I decided to tell him how I felt. He tried to be understanding though I could see how difficult it was for him. This wasn't something he had been called to do. He would have to trust that God was speaking to me on this matter. Halfway around the lake, I spotted something on the ground that looked very colorful. He saw it too. When we got closer, I stooped to pick it up – a purple flowered butterfly teething ring! A baby must have dropped it out of the carriage. Half of its wing had been run over. I looked at Grandpa and we didn't have to say a word. Sharing that feeling of finding the butterfly teething ring just at that moment said it all; God was talking! And not only was God talking, but He had given me the perfect way for "The Butterfly Club" to begin – with a sign of His Divine timing!

CHAPTER 1

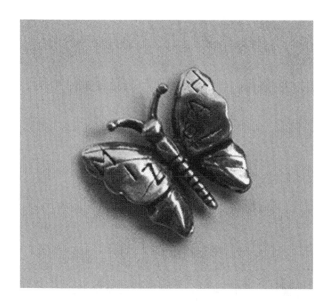

WELCOME TO THE BUTTERFLY CLUB

Hailey, when you go to a wedding or a funeral most likely you will hear this line repeated many times: "It's too bad we only see each other at times like these." While that's only too true, at least we do have those times to catch up with the very large family we have.

It was at one of the family funerals that my cousin, Jackie, sat at our table at the reception afterward. I've always loved Jackie. She was a nurse, caring and dedicated, busy, yet always ready to lend a hand. The last several years had been difficult for her. She grew up in a close-knit family with three siblings: John Paul, the oldest, Madonna, the middle child, and she was the youngest. Her brother, John Paul, was a real sweetheart. He often came to visit your Pépè Phil who had a mission in life to try to get people to quit smoking. Pépè was known to offer $100.00 on the spot if someone would promise to quit cold turkey. John Paul was always a good sport about it, and even though he wasn't one of Pépè's success stories, he always had a soft spot for his Uncle Phil and Aunt Yvonne.

John Paul had found the love of his life, and he and his wife, Nancy, had just had a darling little boy they named Joseph. I was at Pépè's house the day John Paul came to proudly show him off. It was not long after that visit we would learn John Paul had been diagnosed with cancer. It was devastating news and everyone who heard had the same thing to say. "Why does it always happen to the good ones, the special ones in the family that everyone loves so much?" After exhausting treatments and a long battle with leiomyosarcoma, a rare soft tissue cancer, John Paul died two years later; he was 35 years old.

That morning Jackie told me that during John Paul's wake, a man who worked with her dad, who had lost his 17-year-old daughter to leukemia the year before, came through the line wearing a butterfly pin on his lapel. When she and her sister Madonna saw it, they looked at each other and began to tell him what butterflies meant to them. The man smiled and said, "Welcome to the butterfly club," and walked away. Jackie said they wanted to stop him and ask him to explain what that meant, but there were so many people still coming through the line that it was impossible.

At this point, she had really aroused my curiosity. I asked her what butterflies meant to her and Madonna. She had just started to say that they had experienced many butterfly signs surrounding John's death, when one of our aunts interrupted our conversation by asking if she could have a word with her in private. Jackie turned to me and said, "I've written down the butterfly stories, and when I have a chance I'll send them to you."

I never did get the chance to ask her about that man's comment regarding the butterfly club, and Hailey, I can't tell you how many times I thought about it. The name had immediately intrigued me. Was there really an official "Butterfly Club?" What made him welcome Jackie and Madonna into it? I was curious to see the pin. Was it for members only? So many questions

I wanted answered, and it amazes me still, how many years would slip by before I would get back in touch with Jackie again. Then, one day, it was as if nothing could have stopped me from writing to her. I said I was sorry I hadn't followed up on it till now, but would she still be able to send me the butterfly stories? Did she remember the man who was in the line at the wake the day of John Paul's funeral and had welcomed her and Madonna into the butterfly club? Would it be possible for her to arrange for me to meet with him?

I loved her reply. "Phyllis, I can't tell you how many times I've wanted to get back to you with all the butterfly stories. No excuses, life just has happened and time goes by sooo fast." She promised to put the butterfly stories together for me the next day. She wrote that she was guided to start a website and dedicate it to John. She said it was no coincidence that I had emailed her the very day it was up and running. I felt the same way. She had also called her dad to ask for the man's name who had mysteriously welcomed them into the butterfly club. His name was Bob Dagesse. She had reached him but was sorry to say that he and his family were just leaving for the summer and wouldn't be home till Labor Day. I was disappointed for the delay, but pleased that he said he would love to meet with me when he returned. She gave me his phone number and said I should call him. True to her word, I received the butterfly stories that very week, and I couldn't wait to read them.

The Difference Between a Sign and a Coincidence

Hailey, when Jackie's dearest brother, John Paul, was dying and she was trying to make sense of it all, she read a book by Elisabeth Kübler-Ross entitled: "The Wheel of Life, A Memoir of Loving and Dying." The book discusses how when you die you are finally able to shed your cocoon and you fly away like a beautiful butterfly where you feel no pain, sorrow or fear, only peace and love. Jackie thought the butterfly was a great analogy for death and decided she would share it with her two boys who were five and seven years old at the time.

The very next day her son went to a birthday party and a big butterfly flew into the garage. The mom jokingly said, "Excuse me Mr. Butterfly, we didn't invite you to the party." Jackie said she didn't think much of it at the time. The day after that, on a Sunday, she and John Paul went to see Madonna's seven-year-old daughter, Amanda, at her dance recital. She and 10 other little girls were butterflies. It was a very tough day all around as John Paul had been through five weeks of hospitalization in which he was operated on four times. He didn't look very well and couldn't walk very well.

That night, Amanda told her mother that John was going to die. At that point, no one had told John Paul that he was terminal so her mother told her that we're all going to die someday. But Amanda insisted that Uncle John was going to die soon. Madonna told her the analogy of the butterfly by Elisabeth Kübler-Ross, but Amanda had her own ideas on the subject. "No, Mommy," she said, "God's a butterfly and He sits on my shoulder when He talks to me." When her mother asked her why she had never talked about this before, I thought her answer was quite profound. "When God talks to you," she said, "it is very private, mommy." As Amanda continued trying to figure it all out, she said, "God's a butterfly and people are angels. I don't know what happens when you die, but I'll ask God the next time He talks to me."

An unexpected butterfly story followed the next afternoon when Jackie saw her best friend who told her she wasn't going to believe what happened to her at the beach the day before. She was lying on her blanket praying for answers when a 3-inch butterfly landed on her blanket and stayed there for a long time. She told Jackie, "How can you not believe in God when something like that happens?" Hailey, remember when I said that sometimes God speaks to you through another person? Well, Jackie's friend had no idea that Jackie had been struggling to figure out if the butterflies were signs from God or all just a bunch of bizarre coincidences. And here she comes innocently saying, how can you not believe in God when He sends you a butterfly?

Later that evening, when Jackie told her husband about everything, she glanced over at her bedside table and saw the book by Elisabeth Kübler-Ross sitting there. On the cover was a monarch butterfly with flowers all around it that were out of focus so that it made the butterfly really stand out. She noticed three other smaller butterflies on the cover of that book. God was sending her butterflies everywhere.

A week later Jackie went on vacation to Canada with her family, and her mother called to tell her more devastating news about her brother's health: John Paul was paralyzed from the waist down. I remember when our own family got the news. It was so heartbreaking. I couldn't begin to imagine how she must have felt hearing this news about a brother whom she loved so dearly. After the phone call, she was very upset and went for a ride by herself. Driving through a farm area, white butterflies were suddenly everywhere around her car. She saw a big wooden butterfly on the side of the road and painted smaller wooden butterflies were attached to it that you could hang on your house. She bought a purple one to hang on her porch.

After they got back from their vacation, she and her son were coloring together. The page he opened to was a lady with a net catching butterflies. She started coloring them. Her son asked her to show him how to draw a butterfly so he could make a card for his Grandma and Pépè. He drew a bunch of butterflies on the outside and asked his mother to write this inside, "Grandma and Pépè, now you have your own butterflies, Love Jeff." Did that qualify as a sign she wondered?

After supper, Jeff came up to her with a plastic purple butterfly she didn't even know they had. "Look what I found, Mommy," he said. At that point she called Madonna and said, "The butterflies are back."

A few days later Amanda was online at the American Girl website. There is a section where you can go to other girls' websites. She clicked on the name Kristina, which led her to a butterfly website full of colorful butterflies. It also connected her to articles on how butterflies have been spiritual signs for people. Butterfly signs all around...

It was in the middle of July when John Paul was told that he was terminal; there was no more treatment. At that point Jackie talked to his wife, Nancy, and told her all about the butterfly signs. Nancy was in awe. Then she remembered that two years ago, the fall before John was diagnosed, she and John, with little Joseph on her back, went hiking in New Hampshire, and a butterfly followed them all the way to the top of the mountain. They kept turning around because they thought it was so odd. Nancy told Jackie she felt that this was a sign way back then that God was looking out for them, and would continue to do so. Can you imagine the kind of faith, the kind of relationship Nancy had with God, Hailey, to see things in that light as her husband lay dying? When it was time for Joseph to go to bed that night, she read him his favorite book about a chipmunk looking for a home. She had to struggle to see through the tears in her eyes when she and Joseph counted 32 butterflies – 32 butterflies she had never even noticed before. I believe when the connection of God's perfect timing is truly realized, that's the difference between a sign and a coincidence!

Jackie was excited to tell her brother about all of this, but he was skeptical and said it's good for people that believe it. This was really disappointing because she thought it would bring him peace too. Madonna reminded her that the signs were for them and he didn't have to get it. He'd get his own. Not long after that when his Hospice nurse was there, he asked her to wake him up the same way she did that morning. He explained that he was having a wonderful dream. He was on white fluffy pillows and very peaceful and comfortable and she came in with a very gentle voice and said, "Good morning, John." He said, "it was almost spiritual." Then he looked at his sister and said, "Jackie really believes in that stuff." Jackie began to tell the nurse some of the butterfly stories and she thought it was great. John Paul turned to her and listened, and for the first time seemed to believe. The nurse told them that in her church, the First Communion children's sashes have a butterfly on one side and a lamb on the other. The butterfly symbolizes new life and the lamb innocence.

When John Paul died, Nancy requested a butterfly be put in the flower arrangement.

Lots of Butterfly Stories

Hailey, after I told your Uncle Trevor about writing this book, he called to tell me about a story he had heard on the news. It was Mother's Day weekend, and a Little League baseball game had been scheduled for that Saturday. An eight-year-old boy who had just lost his mother to cancer was up at bat. He started to swing the bat to get ready for the first pitch when suddenly there was a flurry of butterflies all around him. Though everyone else had tears streaming down their faces, he was wearing this big grin. He said afterward that he knew the butterflies had come to tell him his mother was in heaven watching him play!

The more I talked to people about their death experiences the more I was amazed to learn how many of them had a story to tell about a butterfly. When Jackie first told me about her butterfly stories I immediately remembered a butterfly story I knew that a dear church friend had shared with me many years ago. Her name was Nancy. The story was about her son, Danny, who was in the same high-school class as your mother.

Danny

You had to love Danny, and not because he was class president, president of the CYO, or the fact that he was the most popular boy in church, school, work, anywhere he was. He just had that winning way about him. No one group could claim him; he crossed over all the youth barriers and was known for his acceptance of everyone. His friendship with many of the less-popular kids made them accepted. Danny was playful and kind. He bounced into church wearing shorts and a scarf around his neck that dropped to his knees. He wore wild Hawaiian shirts and always made you smile.

Danny was outrageous and directed by an inner Spirit that was centered on Jesus. He was 18 when he was struck and killed by a hit-and-run driver as he made his way back to the dorm on his bicycle late one night.

You never forget where you are when you hear such news. When we got the call, Grandpa and I were in the church hall with some members of the community, setting up for the first Lighthouse coffeehouse of the season. We were all in shock; no one could believe what we were hearing. It was three weeks into September. He had barely left for college. Danny, our Danny, had left like the bright foliage of autumn, without our permission, with no control. His death brought on an early winter.

Hailey, the grieving process is a journey with many faces. Helplessly we watched the first stage of anger clutch at his mother's heart as she turned away from God and from the community that tried its best to be there for her. Nancy had three other children to take care of and, as a mother, no one was more aware of how much they needed her than she was. But how do you help your children heal when your own heart seems to have stopped beating?

It was many months later when I bumped into her unexpectedly in the church sanctuary. I was surprised to see the darkness in her eyes had gone and a smile that had been a stranger for so long crossed her lips. She touched my arm and told me that something miraculous had happened to her, something very hard to believe. Nancy shared her pain with me that day. She shared her grieving, her journey. What she told me so touched my heart that I wrote a story about her experience, and I want to share that story with you now Hailey...

"It was only because of what had happened to her in the field that she had the courage to take out the box. Since the moment she heard the news about her son's death, sadness had been her constant companion. But now, even that familiar feeling was gone and replaced with a frightening emptiness. She suddenly realized she couldn't bear to go on.

"She spent the morning walking aimlessly in a near-by meadow when she was stopped abruptly by a huge fallen log. One whole length of it had smooth bark that beckoned her to sit. So she sat, noticing the long branch in the center of it reaching up like an arm to-ward the sky. Her intention to close the world out was broken by the interruption of a butterfly that caught her eye and landed on the branch. It was a monarch and seemed to be drunk the way it hovered around her a little too closely. It was insistent, not leaving her side until she was completely drawn to it. Her heart started to match the flutter of this small winged creature as it stirred up the air out of all proportion to its size. Then it landed on a small stick near her feet. She bent down and unconsciously held her breath as she picked up the stick, because somehow she knew before it hap-pened that the butterfly would not fly away. Holding it in her hands, it was as if her son Danny was speaking the words himself, "Mom, it's okay. I'm alright." She knew now what others had spoken of, what words could not convey. In the mystery of death, Danny had been allowed to surround her with his presence so she could go on.

"The next morning, as soon as her three children left for school, she had taken out the box with Danny's name on it. Filled with boyhood treasures that brought back the moments of his life, she touched them and touched him in the process. She read each card. She saved the written journal until last. She cried until she could cry no more.

"Nothing with the family had been the same since the day Danny died. She watched how each of her children was affected differently and prayed to find ways to allow them to express their grief and begin the healing process. She had made her decision when she held the butterfly in her hands. The family would decorate the house and celebrate Christmas the way they always had. She knew that as long as the children avoided the family traditions, the rituals that Danny had always been a part of, somehow they could continue to live in denial of his death.

"She had the Christmas boxes in the living room when they came home with the tree. They decorated it like a chore she had insisted they do. She shared their pain of placing the ornaments that spoke of the four of them. Only at her direction did they hang the four stockings on the mantel in order of birth: Danny, Rachel, Joey and Bobby.

"She didn't know where the words came from but they came. "We'll all write messages to Danny and put them in his stocking," she said. As the days passed, Danny's stocking was filled with small notes and longer letters that were the aching of the missed conversations, the plans and secrets whispered in rooms this time of year.

"They set up their precious heirloom Nativity on Christmas Eve. The family went to the Christmas Eve pageant. Faithful Bridgett, the donkey, carried Mary down the aisle, Joseph by her side. The church was filled with angel wings and shepherd's staffs, all part of the live gospel drama that unfolded each year. It was filled with Danny.

"Somehow during the early hours of the morning the stockings got filled. She touched the letters in Danny's stocking. They were not for her to read, but she heard the sound of Christmas in them. She sat on the floor before the baby in their manger. She understood what Danny came to tell her. It was all there in the story of the butterfly. Danny was alive, only changed and wrapped in a new glory. In time, her three children would see that's what the letters were saying; there would always be four children, and four Christmas stockings."

Nancy realized that as powerful and life changing as this sign had been to her, some people would dismiss it as simply a coincidence. It is ironic, really, that when you make the connection of God's perfect timing through a sign, you want to share it with everyone because it is so wondrous. And at the same time you are only too aware how you cannot make anyone feel the undeniable presence of God you felt at the moment you received the sign. For me, Hailey, for those who truly wished they could have real proof that the butterfly was a sign from God, Nancy herself was the proof. The radical change and new heart she received from God that day was impossible for anyone to deny.

CHAPTER 2

Not just butterflies, but...

After Ira died, I asked your mom if she had ever experienced a sign from God surrounding his death. There were no butterflies, but she said several things had happened, though she didn't know if they would qualify as real signs. I asked her if she'd write them down. When she did, I think she got her answer.

Hailey, your mother is one of the kindest, most generous, good people I know. It was never hard for her to believe in God. Part of the reason, I'm sure, is because God was so much a part of her. Of course she had her questions just like everyone else, but she always knew God in her heart. And so I was particularly interested to read her experiences after Ira died, and I'll always keep the yellow construction paper she hand wrote this on...

"My brother-in-law passed away on June 13, 2002. He was 32 years old. His death was sudden and tragic. It poured the first three days after his car accident and then the sun came out, as if to try to dry our tears on the day he was laid to rest.

"When Ira died I was desperate for a sign from him. I could feel him around me, but I wanted a physical, tangible sign that he still existed somehow. I would have settled for an icy cold passing through my body, an object being lifted before me or, mostly, his ghostly form appearing before me, if only to see him one more time.

"Ira had this dog named Jenna who he lovingly called his "lap dog". She was of medium build, above-average intelligence, and had one blue eye and one brown. She was his baby. The morning of his wake I wandered aimlessly through the aisles of our local video store looking for a movie for my three-and-a-half year old daughter, Hailey. The very first movie we picked up was about a husky dog. As I was reading the back of the video the name "Jenna" popped out at me. It was about a rescue dog named Jenna. Was this a sign or just a simple coincidence?

"A few days after the funeral I took Hailey to the park. The woman next to me was pushing her little girl on the swings. I was busy with my thoughts when the woman's voice calling, "Jenna," wakened me abruptly from my reverie. Was it just the phenomenon like when you buy a certain car and then you suddenly see it everywhere or were these subtle messages?

"One day around Christmas Hailey and I went to the library. I was searching through craft books to find a project idea to celebrate New Year's. There wasn't a lot on the topic in general and even less for craft ideas. I finally flipped to a page about making cards or a collage with paper plates. My heart skipped a beat and my eyes brimmed with tears as I read the words that were written in the middle of the sample card: "Happy New Year, Love Ira." Now Jenna may be a name you hear now and then but I have never met another Ira, except for my father-in-law. We didn't spend a lot of holidays with Ira because he worked most of them, but we always had celebrated every New Year's Eve together. I wanted to think that was his way of still coming to our party.

"My mother-in-law always decorated Ira's grave with a variety of special mementos depending on the season. On Christmas she put a small stuffed animal dog that wore a Santa hat and was reminiscent of Jenna. When spring arrived the stuffed animal was brought home and put in a special place at his parents' house. Ira's aunt came to visit. We all gathered around a radio CD player to listen to a song about grieving. As the beautiful voice echoed through the room and into tender hearts, in walked Jenna carrying this special Santa dog in her mouth. Jenna was now close to ten years old and never touched things that weren't part of her overwhelming pile of dog toys.

"I have never received my physical, 'hit me over the head here I am sign.' I've sat on his grave and prayed and searched the eyes of his portrait that hangs on our wall. 'Are you here?' I ask. 'Is there an afterlife?' I haven't received a verbal answer to these questions. But sometimes I think, that while I've asked for signs I've refuted what signs I've been given as coincidence. I could rationalize all of these happenings away with simple explanations. But the truth is, Ira was made present before me again and that's really what I had asked for."

Hailey, those signs happened right after Ira died, and your mom said she continued to feel Ira's presence in myriad ways through all these many years. When it was coming up on the 10th anniversary of Ira's death, Memaw had a celebration cook out with "her boys" as she lovingly referred to them; the old friends from the neighborhood. Trevor and Dawn were there and everyone got to meet Ella Grace and Jack Lincoln, their children. The boys were touched to learn that Trevor and his wife, Dawn, had given Jack Ira's middle name. Memaw had an album of pictures for all of us to enjoy, and each of us had our own Ira stories to tell. It was a wonderful remembrance of Ira's life. One would think if God were going to send a sign from Ira He would have chosen that day. But I find that God likes to send a sign when it's least expected, as if He enjoys the surprise of it all. For that reason, your mom never expected the sign she got the following year on the 11th anniversary of Ira's death; a sign that let her know he's definitely still around.

She was reading one of her favorite author's murder mysteries and came across a line in the book that gave her chills straight through her body and made her reread the line several times. The detectives were attempting to decipher the significance of a number pattern that was left at a crime scene and they wondered if the numbers could have been a person's birth date until the day they died. Normally, when you are looking at a person's date of birth till the date of death, you would see the year included too. It just goes hand in hand. For example, January 4, 1950 – June 13, 2003. But mysteriously, only these two dates were being looked at – January 4 and June 13 – no year. Hailey, your dad was born on January 4th and Ira died on June 13th. Your mom said when she made the connection the air in the room swirled of memories held near and times that could have been. Ira's presence was palpable, as though he were standing in the room right then, smiling. He was sending signs not only to her, but knowing she would pass them along to your dad, to you, his little pal who had grown up to be such an attractive niece, and to Caleb who was too young to have any memories of his own. Your mother said it so perfectly; the gift of God's signs is that they really bring life once again.

Ira's Here

For the past several years, Grandpa and I had tried to plan a day to go to the Brimfield Fair in May with Trevor. You know how they both have an eye for antiques. But for one reason or another it just didn't work out for Trevor to make it. Some years Grandpa and I would go on our own. That particular year, plans were made again and this time it was Grandpa who couldn't make it. I was happy when it worked out for Trevor and me to go anyway. And if it hadn't worked out just that way we never would have had the conversation we did.

It was a pleasant drive to Sturbridge, such a lovely day, and I enjoyed listening to Trevor tell me some cute and funny stories about what Ella said or what Jack did. He is so proud of them, and such a loving father. He knew I was working on this book, and after a while, he asked me how it was coming along. I explained the overall plan and he wanted to hear about some of the stories I had already written. When I mentioned that I was including Ira's story, I asked him if Jessie had ever had a chance to tell him about the signs she had received from Ira after he died. He said no, he and Jessie had never talked about Ira's dying, but he was very interested to hear about the signs she had experienced. Afterward, I could tell it meant a lot to him.

Trevor, like your dad, did not like to talk about Ira; it brought up too many painful memories. His feelings concerning him were so private that they couldn't surface in ordinary conversation; they needed a gifted space such as we had that day. I was deeply moved and thankful for this chance to hear Trevor share his feelings now. As we drove, he told me that he had experienced several signs from Ira too. No one else could capture what he had to say like he did that morning. I asked him if he would write it all down for me. This is the telling of the three signs Ira sent to him in your Uncle Trevor's own words. It was no surprise that Ira's three signs to Trevor would all involve music.

Have You Seen Junior's Grades?

"Ira was about three years older than me. When you are an adult, three years is nothing. But when you are twelve, three years is everything. I was at the age where I had just started listening to my own kind of music. It was the early 1980's and I was listening to hard rock bands like Def Leppard, Motley Crue and Van Halen. I had just gotten Van Halen's 1984 album and listened to it non-stop on my Walkman. Everyone has heard of Van Halen now, but back then they were just starting to get popular, at least in the suburbs of Massachusetts.

"The older kids ruled our neighborhood. We looked up to them with fear and as role models. Some more for the former and some more for the latter. Ira was one of the cool kids and, best of all, one of the nice ones. At age fifteen to our twelve, he was someone we felt special to get to hang around with when we could. We wanted to be like him, do the things he did, listen to the music he listened to.

"Ira was of course into Van Halen like we all were, but, since he was cool, he had heard of them way before we had. One of his favorite VH albums was 'Woman and Children First' which had come out in 1980 (when I was eight). There is a song on that album, 'And the Cradle Will Rock,' that we especially liked. It is about a kid who would have run in the same crowds as we did and whose plights we could relate to. In one part of the song the lead singer says in a mock authoritative voice, "Have you seen Junior's grades?" Ira used to say this all the time when the song was playing and when it wasn't. I can still see him with his too long 80's style feathered hair, Army jacket, tilting head down, raising an eyebrow, deep voice, 'Have you seen Junior's grades?'

"When Ira died, his parents asked me to pick out the music for his wake. I was told the music would be playing throughout the whole wake so I went through his CD collection and picked out about 20 discs for them to play. During the wake, I noticed that they were not playing music. I didn't say anything of course but wondered what had happened. After the priest had said his final words and we were all getting up to leave, a song started. Apparently the funeral director had decided it was better to just have one song play as we exited. As the opening guitar riff of 'And the Cradle Will Rock' began, I got a chill. I was walking out of the room in the semi-dazed state that a wake will leave you in and the words echoed in my head as they bounced off the walls of the funeral parlor...

'Have you seen Junior's grades?' And Ira, the cool kid, lives on!"

A Concert of Mourning?

"Like a lot of people, Ira and I were big fans of Guns N'Roses during the late 1980's and early 1990's. We both bought the first GNR album as soon as it came out and sat glued to MTV whenever they played the Welcome to the Jungle video, and we were hooked on the band for life.

"I'm kind of obsessive when I get into something, but Ira took that to a whole other level. We ended up going to record shows searching for collectibles, hard to find CD's, albums, and what have you. These were the days before eBay and Google so it was fairly difficult to come across some of this stuff. We took many trips into Boston and Cambridge scouring through bins in obscure record shops for bootlegs of live concerts, unreleased material, imports, anything. Whatever we could find we would just eat up.

"Besides our obsessive natures, finding bootleg material was a necessity because, as any GNR fan will tell you, there had been no new official material released since they had put out an album of cover songs in 1993.

"Axl Rose, the reclusive and temperamental singer, had reportedly been working on a new studio album, but it was taking forever. Literally. It actually became a running joke among fans and pop culture press in general. Reported release dates would come and go with nothing to show for it. It came to a point where Dr. Pepper pledged to give away a free can of soda to every single person in the United States if Axl released the album at any point during the year (2008), in which he claimed that this time it really would be ready.

"Ira died in 2002 and never saw the release of Chinese Democracy (2008), the long awaited GNR album.

"When someone close to you dies, after the initial shock wears off a bit, you sometimes go a while and the pain of their passing, while still there, isn't so strong or immediate. You continue to live your life and go to work and do the things that people do. There are moments though when all the feelings, memories, emotions come rushing back and that pain is very fresh and real again. These feelings are a mixed blessing for me as they hurt but at the same time you feel close to that person again. Or rather, they feel close to you. You see them in your dreams and things are like they used to be and you can somehow spend just a little more time with them.

"When the GNR album finally came out and the band went on tour all I thought about was how excited Ira would have been and how much fun we would have had listening to the new album, going to the concert, looking for collectible merchandise. I felt like, as with so many other things that reminded me of him, the experience of the album release was diminished for me and tainted with the sadness of his not being a part of it.

"When the GNR tour came to our area, my wife and I went to see them. I was excited to see them but Ira's memory made it seem more like a time of mourning than of the fun one would expect going to a concert. My loving wife, who doesn't really like concerts, was clearly there to provide emotional support.

"I had gone in thinking about how Ira was missing this event and this experience and how much he would have enjoyed it. But instead of missing it he was there with us. Unmistakably. He was in the seat next to us and above us and surrounding us. In a comforting and very real way.

"About half-way through the concert the guitarist came out to do his solo. This was a new guitarist, Buckethead, whom I had never seen live. Apparently he was known for wearing an expressionless plain white mask and a KFC bucket on his head (thus his stage name). Rather an odd sight.

"As I watched Buckethead perform his solo I was thinking about Ira and hoping he was enjoying the music we had both waited so long for. At that moment Buckethead happened to walk to the side of the stage where we were sitting and I looked from the blank, black eyes of his mask up at his KFC bucket to see the word 'Funeral' in black letters written across it."

Hailey, could there possibly have been a more perfect sign for Trevor that night than seeing the word "Funeral" written in black letters across a white bucket when he went to the concert carrying all the memory of Ira's dying? I wish you could have seen his face when he was describing that moment to me. I couldn't help but smile to think how much fun Ira would have had telling this story. But then again, maybe he just did!

"Sweet Child O'Mine"

"It was our daughter's first birthday party, and we wanted everything to be perfect. Our first child's first birthday. Both families were getting together for the party and we wanted to make a good impression. Make our parents proud; show everyone the kind of nice family we were becoming.

"Our daughter, Ella, wore a new party dress, my wife and I were both dressed casually, but nice casual. The house was sparkling clean and bright. A local top forties station softly played uncontroversial background music.

"Various appetizers were being set up and the guests were beginning to arrive. My parents, my wife's mother and father, a few uncles and aunts had trickled in. My wife and I were both scrambling around the kitchen trying to get last minute food prep done. People making general small talk. The families still trying to get to know one another. Small talk.

"As I walked past the radio the Guns N'Roses song Sweet Child O'Mine just happened to be starting. For no reason at all, my hand reached down and cranked the volume up as high as it would go. As all conversation around me stopped and various family members (in-laws and outlaws alike) stared at me, I thought to myself, that was an odd thing to do, I wonder why I just did that?

"No sooner had I turned the volume down to a normal level when Ira's parents walked in the room. And I just smiled to myself and said 'Ira's here!'

Hailey, God also spoke to your Memaw and Pop that day of Ella's party. Sometimes, when a person dies, it's difficult to know how to handle it, exactly what you should say. I remember when a dear friend I worked with had lost her husband suddenly. I didn't know if I should talk about him or not. One day I asked her how she felt about it. She said most of her friends never mentioned her husband and this was very hurtful to her. I told her it was hard for people to know what to do. I had wondered if talking about him made the pain worse. She said she thought about him every minute whether people talked about him or not. And it felt good when someone did talk about him; it felt good to remember. I know that's how your Memaw and Pop feel. They love to talk about their son, so we talk about Ira all the time.

One day we were telling stories about him and Memaw mentioned Ella's first birthday party. She said she and Pop had just walked in the foyer at Trevor and Dawn's that day when suddenly a Guns N'Roses song started blasting on the radio. It only lasted a second she said. By the time they had walked in the room where everyone was, the music had already been turned down. She said she looked at Pop and whispered, "Ira's here for sure!" And Hailey, I guess he most certainly was!

Waiting Patiently in Retrospect

Hailey, when Jackie shared her butterfly signs with John Paul's wife, Nancy, she remembered the butterfly that had followed them all the way to the top of the mountain two years before John was even diagnosed. When she made the connection, it made her feel that God was with them back then. That butterfly was a sign of reassurance and comfort patiently waiting for her to discover when she needed it most.

Ira's favorite vacation spot was Jackson, New Hampshire. He went to Nordic Village on his honeymoon and often returned for vacations. The year after Ira died your mom and dad took you and Caleb to Nordic Village. Ira's memory was everywhere. While you were there you went to visit StoryLand. When I was almost finished writing this book, I asked your dad if he had ever had a sign from Ira. He said no. I actually saw the connection being made on Caleb's face as he turned to him and said, "Dad, remember that time we went to StoryLand right after Ira died and a big butterfly landed on your toe and stayed there for a while, and we all thought that was kind of weird? Mom even took a picture of it!" he said. Your mom said she had forgotten all about it. Then she recalled your dad was wearing his favorite flip flops when the butterfly had landed on his big toe, and stayed there long enough for her to get her camera and take that picture. You and Caleb were very excited but your dad still didn't have any recollection of any of this happening. Your mom promised she would find the picture of the butterfly and show it to him, which she did. You smiled at your dad and said he did have a sign after all. But Hailey, I really believe that butterfly sign was a gift from Ira to you and Caleb, patiently waiting in God's divine timing of retrospect for you to remember it and make the connection. Would you agree?

CHAPTER 3

THE DIVINE FORTUNE COOKIE

When Pépè Phil was very sick, you asked me if you thought he could say hi to Ira for you when he got to heaven. I loved how you knew that there was a heaven, and that your Pépè was going there.

Pépè Phil was a good man who helped countless people in his lifetime. He found jobs for them, places to live, and hooked them up to what they needed, as he used to say. He trusted people no one else would trust, often to Nana's dismay. I remember two brothers who were kind of shady characters and sort of friends with one of my brothers. Pépè gave them both a job when he owned his excavating business, and caught one of them stealing from him. "Don't worry about it, Yvonne," he'd say with a twinkle in his eye. "I buy enough shovels and rakes for us and some for them to steal."

All the time they worked for Pépè he'd give them plenty of speeches to try to steer them in the right direction. But the younger brother finally got into some real trouble and wound up in jail. About a year later he called Pépè. He had used his family up and simply had no one else to call. If he could just get a job he told Pépè, he would be able to get out on parole. He begged Pépè to give him one more chance. Pépè called a friend of his and talked him into giving him a job as a mechanic. Years later he surprised Pépè with a visit. He said he wanted him to know that he'd never forget that day when he told him he believed in him; when he looked into his eyes and told him not to let him down. That day had changed his life forever. He went on the straight and narrow, got married and worked hard to support his family. In fact, he was still working at that same job after all this time. Pépè shrugged it off and said it was nothing.

I always loved to hear the stories Pépè had to tell. The first Thanksgiving he and Nana were married they decided to give the turkey Nana got at work to a family who had 12 children. They used to roll pennies back then but still managed to scrape up enough money to also buy the fixings to go with it. When Pépè delivered milk for a dairy in Woonsocket he was told to bring back the cases of those delicious pint containers of chocolate and coffee milk that were left over. It was their policy to pour any leftover milk right down the drain—perfectly good milk. But Pépè would always say, "That was their policy." His policy was stopping on the route home and handing out the milk to the especially needy families he knew of – all with large families. I remember years later when your mom and Trevor were teenagers, one of the men Pépè used to give milk to stopped him at a store. He said he just had to thank him again for that milk. It saw him through the hard times and he'd never forget what he had done for him. Pépè said he couldn't believe the man even remembered. He told me what he always said at times like this, "Aw, that was nothing, Phyl."

He said the same thing when he sold ice cream and stopped on the way home to give out popsicles to the kids on the street. He had a soft spot for kids, and I had witnessed his soft heart many times myself. Nana and Pépè ran a fish-and-chip place when I was growing up. At eight o'clock on a Friday night, after the lines had gone, several families came to the restaurant to pick up the boxes of food Nana had carefully packed for them; fish and chips, fish cakes, cole slaw, enough to feed those families of eight, ten and thirteen. "For the kids," Pépè would say. And many times when I was just a kid myself and Pépè would take me to the store and give me a nickel to spend, he'd hand out a pocket full of nickels to any of the kids lucky enough to be near him. And Hailey, a nickel could buy quite a lot of candy in those days.

Pépè died at home when you were seven. Caleb was five. It was his wish to die at home and we made that our promise to him. We did it with the help of hospice and a care calendar; the six of us, his three girls and three boys, and all of our children, made the commitment to be there around the clock to care for him. Terri, my brother Dicky's wife, brought over her delicious home-made meals four or five times a week. Nana had done it all for as long as she could, but she was slowly wearing out. For me it was especially heartwarming to see the grandchildren filling up the time slots as much as they could. It warmed my heart to see Jared, 18 years old then, sit by Pépè's bedside and hold his hand. I bet you can just picture that; you know how sweet Jared is. Sometimes, when I came in for one of the night shifts, he'd be doing the dishes to give Nana a break. If he was headed out afterward with a friend, he'd bring along his friend to the house. Pépè who barely weighed 100 pounds would whisper in his gravel voice, "Jared, make sure your friend has something to eat."

I remember Phil, 17, coming in one afternoon just as Pépè had to go to the bathroom. He could hardly stand at that point, never mind walk, yet he still insisted on trying. Phil got him up and said, "Pep, I'll carry you on my back if I have to." I cried softly in the other room. They all helped. Jill and Alanna taking their shifts; always willing to take an extra shift whenever you needed them to. Madi and Justin were young then but patiently played games with Pépè for hours making him laugh until he just couldn't play anymore. You and Caleb, Pépè's only great grandchildren till Ella was born that July, always visited by his bedside. When you kissed his cheek, he'd tell you he loved you, and then he would take your hand and tell you it made him feel better.

Pépè died on Friday, September 8, 2006 at 3:33 in the afternoon. We were all there around his bedside. My older sister Mary had been scheduled for the overnight shift the night before, but for some reason we had switched. Hailey, I had never seen anyone die before so I didn't know what to expect even though I knew it wouldn't be long.

The six of us, Mary, Jacky, John, Dicky, Jerry and I, each had our different and unique relationship with

Pépè, and between all of us we had what was needed to meet his many needs. My gift, I believe, was prayer. Pépè was never one to talk about his faith or outwardly show it, yet, in the last months of his life, we prayed the rosary together and I blessed him every night before he went to sleep. Sometimes I'd ask him if he wanted me to read the Bible to him and he would nod his head yes. It seemed to bring him a lot of comfort. One night I asked him if he was afraid to die. When he hesitated I quickly added, "you do know you're going to heaven." He tightened his lips and tilted his head the way he used to when he was still trying to figure something out. "My dear Papa," I told him, "you have lived your whole life as an example of the Good Samaritan in the parable Jesus told, and I know Jesus has prepared a place for you." I read him the story of the Good Samaritan and for a long time told him the stories we all knew of all the people he had helped in his lifetime. "You are the Good Samaritan," I whispered to him. He squeezed my hand, and tears sprang up in his eyes.

The morning before Pépè died, he asked me to get him a drink but every drink I brought him from juice to lemonade to water seemed to taste like poison in his mouth. I put the glass to his lips but he just couldn't swallow it, not even a sip. He had been eating pudding and mashed scramble eggs for a while but now he was choking on anything. He was in and out of consciousness all day. That night, as I slept on the cot near his hospital bed, which was center stage in the living room like he always was, I heard such a loud gurgling in his throat that I was afraid he would actually drown. That thought really frightened me. I called the hospice number and spoke to a doctor. He told me to hold the phone near his throat so he could listen. "Call the family in," he said, "it won't be long now." It was two thirty in the morning.

Grandpa was there in five minutes. Mary was the next to arrive from Boston and Jacky soon followed from Beverly. Soon all his children were there gathered around his bedside while the older grandchildren came in one by one as their parents called them. It was strange, we wanted to gently rub his hands to let him know we were there with him, but the hospice nurses had told us not to touch him. They explained that at the very end his nerves would be so sensitive that it would actually hurt him. However, they assured us that he could still hear us. Through the night we told him all the family stories, sleeping here and there for 15 or 20 minutes at a time. By ten o'clock the next morning Pépè was still gurgling. He was so ready to die. He had asked me many times to tell God to take him and couldn't understand why He didn't. One of the nurses told us that maybe he was holding on for one of us to say something he needed to hear before he died. But Hailey, we all had had our chance to thank him for being such a good father and to tell him we loved him. We were grateful for that. And like the hospice nurses had guided us to do, we also told him, and Nana did too, that it was alright for him to go now. Then, at three thirty-three in the afternoon, while we were all gathered around his bedside, he took three deep breaths, his eyes opened wide, and he exhaled for the last time. He was gone. And it had happened so peacefully. As the afternoon sun's rays streamed in through the open windows in that still room, we could feel his spirit tangibly lifting from his body. God was taking him. One by one we kissed him goodbye for the last time, and my heart nearly broke as Trevor bent down to kiss him with little Ella, just six weeks old, in his arms. I remembered how Pépè kept rubbing Ella's little head when Dawn and Trevor had stopped by to visit on their way home from the hospital just after she was born. How Pépè would have loved to see her grow up! Like all of you, she would have been his little pumpkin.

Funeral arrangements were decided. There would be a wake and a private service the next day just for the family. I would do the eulogy. There was no doubt in my mind which reading I would choose: the parable of the Good Samaritan. Reading that to him and reminding him of how he had lived those words Jesus taught had brought him so much comfort. And it would bring us comfort now to know that Pépè's life surely warranted the promise of what was needed to inherit eternal life. There was yet another reason I wanted to share that parable. I wanted to remind my brothers and sisters of the story that happened to us when we were kids, and how my father literally had been the Good Samaritan Jesus described in that parable.

Pépè was driving us home in our station wagon. We were following a pickup truck with a bunch of kids in wet bathing suits all in the back bed of the truck. That nice summer day had suddenly turned dark and cold and it was pouring. The road was narrow and slippery. We never did find out why the driver had to slam on his brakes but, when he did, all the kids went flying out of the truck and onto the road. Pépè stopped behind them. Thankfully, there were only a few houses on our road then and hardly any traffic. When Pépè got out of the car he saw bloody bodies scattered in the road. One of the kids had his teeth knocked out. There were no cell phones in those days, and Pépè said they needed to get to the hospital right away. The frantic driver was saying something to my father and I heard Pépè say, "Don't worry, I'll take care of everything if I have to." He got in the front seat with my father, and we all shifted places to make room. Remember Hailey, there were no seat belts then. The youngest one in the family would always stand on the seat very close to my father. If he had to stop fast he would put his arm out to keep you from falling. That was our seat belt. Someone always rode in the way back of the station wagon. That was my favorite place, especially if we were driving a little distance. I'd sit cross-legged or lie down with one leg up and the other one crossed over the knee. And we'd sing songs back there and share our secrets. That day, however, I was in the middle seat and will never forget those bloodied kids being lifted in the car with us. It was a really tight squeeze, arms and legs everywhere. Today, we know better than to lift someone who has been in an accident. Fortunately, it all worked out fine and everyone involved was very grateful for my father's help. Pépè was indeed the Good Samaritan. When I told the family I would like to use the parable of the Good Samaritan for the prayer service, they were open to the idea, and I was happy to have this story to share.

The Saturday and Sunday after Pépè died, we worked on several huge collages that my sister Jacky and sister-in-law Lynne put together with Jessie's help as well. They were beautiful and told the story in pictures, poems and heartfelt phrases of "a farmer and his wife." It began with their wedding picture and ended with the last picture of Pépè rubbing Ella's head when she had come to visit at three days old.

Emily wrote the words for the prayer card given out at wakes. Emily is Jacky's daughter, my younger sister, who lives in Beverly. She is the next oldest grandchild, ten years younger than your mom. She moved to Oregon when you were just little. What she wrote perfectly captured Pépè's life:

In Loving Memory of
Philip L. Vadenais
June 15, 1926 – September 8, 2006

My life is made up of the hundreds
of photos that line these walls.
Thousands of meals have been born
from this oven. The floor is worn
from all of your footsteps. The
windows have brightened even the
saddest of times, and the doors have
welcomed every visitor. The air is
filled with your voices. This is my
home. Let me go in peace. Let me
slip away while the photos on the
wall stand still. Let the smell of
your last cooked meal linger, and
the tender touch of your hands calm
mine. Let me look at you while I
say goodbye. Let me say goodbye in
my home.

The wake was not until Tuesday night. On Sunday Jacky returned to Beverly, Mary to Boston, and I stayed with Nana during the day on Monday. Your mom's block of time was Monday night. Every week for months now it had been a tradition for her to bring Chinese food for their supper. It was a real treat for Nana because

Pépè never liked Chinese food. That night, after they finished eating, Nana opened her fortune cookie. She couldn't see without her glasses and asked your mother to read it to her. Jessie couldn't believe what the fortune said. "The Good Samaritan did not get his name through good intentions." She called me immediately. And quickly the story went out through the family grapevine. We were all totally amazed. There was no doubt, Hailey, God had sent this message to tell us Pépè Phil was in heaven, just like you knew all along!

CHAPTER 4

That's god talking

"Can God talk to us?" you asked that night in the van on our way to LaSalette. And I tell you, dear Hailey, that I cannot stop marveling at how He does! Consider how your mom had been bringing Chinese food to Nana on Monday nights for so many months. Then, on the very Monday night before the wake, and only after the family knew that the parable of the Good Samaritan would be the reading for his service, Nana opened a fortune cookie that was about the Good Samaritan. Think of all those fortune cookies in a huge jar, all the people getting take-out that night, and that one cookie was put in your mother's bag.

Consider also that Grandpa and I have been taking your mom and Trevor to Chinese restaurants since they were born, and we all still go every chance we can! In all that time we could have gotten that fortune cookie. But we didn't until that night. Ask yourself how many times in all those lunches, over all those years, have any of us ever opened a fortune cookie that referenced the scriptures? That night when your mom read Nana's fortune, her heart jumped in her chest the same way it had when she read that sample card: "Happy New Year, Love Ira." It jumped because she made the connection. She recognized God talking to her. And how else can God talk to us when God is a spirit?

Did you know that Grandpa and I have been walking around our lovely lake nearly every day for over thirty years? And the very day we found the butterfly teething ring was the day I felt compelled to tell Grandpa that I knew God was wanting me to begin writing this book. Not the day before. Not the day after. The very same day! There never was a butterfly toy before or since.

God uses divine timing to speak to us in a way we can understand; a very personal, intimate way. And think how perfect the circumstances have to be for God to communicate with us through a sign. For example, Trevor was asked to pick out music for Ira's wake. Because he was told they would be playing music throughout the entire wake, he picked out 20 CD's from Ira's collection. Without his knowing, plans were changed afterward, and only one song was played as the people exited the funeral parlor. If Trevor had been asked in the first place to pick out only one song, he would have picked out Ira's favorite song himself, and there would have been no opportunity for a sign. But the way it happened, out of the 20 CD's and that's a lot of songs, without being told, the funeral director played Ira's favorite song; the song he always quoted. When Grandpa and I heard that song on our way out of the funeral home that day, we assumed like everyone else that it was being played because Ira liked that kind of music. But to Trevor, who knew the circumstances of that particular song being chosen, it was a sign that told him, "Ira's here." One day you do find yourself asking, how many coincidences have to happen before it is not a coincidence?

I believe it was no coincidence that when I finally wrote to Jackie to get Bob Dagesse's number and make plans to meet with him, he was going to be away for several months. I had so many questions I wanted to ask him, but there wasn't a thing I could do to rush it. In the interim I had all this time on my hands to think, and think I did. As the days passed, signs and stories I had experienced in my own life or seen happen in other people's lives, would suddenly pop into my mind. The first one was a butterfly sign; the one I shared with you about Danny. Other signs like the fortune cookie, the "funeral hat," the music, the New Year's Eve card, even the special Santa dog, were also signs connected to a loved one dying. But there were many more signs I had witnessed where God had definitely talked to someone. Sometimes to inspire or encourage. Other times to comfort or affirm. To motivate, to whisper, "It's time." One sign even literally hit a man over the head! During those months Bob was away I began to gather these stories. I want to share them with you now, Hailey, as we wait together for Bob's return.

A Postcard From God

Hailey, I think there are many young people who get discouraged thinking the world is just too big for anyone to make a difference. Grandpa and I were meeting with the Confirmation Class at our church to help them realize how our community was reaching out together to make a difference, and we wanted them to feel they were a part of it too.

We began our presentation by describing the seven places our church was currently tithing to, and shared a little bit about the person or people who had dedicated their lives to serving God. We talked about their goals, what they were doing to change people's lives, what assistance they provided, etc. It was wonderful to see how interested our young people were. We asked each student to choose one of the postcards that were pre-addressed to the seven places we tithed to. Their task was to write a message of gratitude and encouragement to the person running the program. This proved to be harder than they expected, especially for one boy. He sat there intermittently tapping the pen on his desk. Said he wasn't good at that kind of thing. At the end of class he managed to scribble out this one line: "Yo, I'm really proud of the work that you're doing!" When I read what he had written it made me smile, and at the same time, his vulnerability touched something deep within my heart.

Sometimes our community was blessed to be able to invite someone who ran one of the programs to be our guest speaker for our adult religious education program. It was a real surprise to learn that Father Fred, who ran our mission church in Haiti, actually came home every other year to visit his elderly parents. This was his year to come home, and he was only too happy to accept our invitation to celebrate Mass and speak to our community. As he stood at the pulpit to give the homily, his words were like a video through which we saw his mountain village in Carice, and he described the major role we played in the people's lives there. He used our tithe for many purposes and sometimes he was able to hire the men to work different jobs where they could feel they were supporting their family. Though they tried so hard to get ahead, the political corruption viciously bound the people to a state of poverty.

We had no way of knowing that for the past year Father Fred was discouraged himself. Was he really making a difference? After all his time there the poverty was virtually the same. His 25th anniversary as a priest was fast approaching and he began to really ask God what He wanted him to do. Should he stay or was it time to transfer somewhere else?" "For one month the inner nagging continued," he confided. "But God answers our prayers, eh? And I remember the day he answered mine." Hailey, you could have heard a pin drop in the church that morning as Father Fred told us how God had actually talked to him. "It was so hot. Well, it's always hot in Haiti," he said smiling. "But it was a rare moment for me to be alone in my makeshift office. Usually, from the moment I arrive, so do the people, each with a different problem to resolve. And maybe it happens sometimes like this for you, but as soon as I am alone, those thoughts you try to bury suddenly find their way to the surface. 25 years and nothing seems to have changed. I looked up in despair and said the words out loud, "God, do you really want me to continue my work here in Haiti?"

"With the words still ringing in the air I was interrupted by the mail. Here, let me read what I received." He drew a postcard from his pocket and held it in the air. "Yo, I'm really proud of the work that you're doing!" And there being no signature, well, who else could I think it was from except God? I must admit I was a bit surprised at the language He chose, but after all, these are modern times!" He flashed his boyish grin while the community laughed despite the tears springing in their eyes. "And it wasn't until two days later that I started receiving other postcards, and only then realized they were notes of encouragement from you, my dear friends in the States. And to think you had no way of knowing how much I was in need of some good news." He put the rest of the postcards in his shirt pocket. "I guess you just never know how God will use us, eh?" he said.

Hailey, I thought about the boy in our class and Father Fred and what had happened for a long time afterward. What were the odds that with all those different postcards piled up on the table addressed to seven different places, that boy would choose the one addressed to Haiti? All the postcards were mailed at the post office the same day. Yet, we would learn how the postcards arrived at different days at all the places we mailed to. How did it happen that this young boy's postcard would be the one to arrive in Haiti two days before the rest? And even the fact that we had been tithing to that Mission for several years and only found out that year that Father Fred came home to visit his parents; the very year he needed some encouragement. The very year his 25th anniversary had brought him to a crossroad in his life. I also thought how that young student perhaps felt that what he wrote wasn't as good as the others. And yet, God chose his words to communicate to Father Fred. I guess Father Fred was right. You just never know how God will use us. And you never know how God will choose to talk to us, eh?"

The Collection Basket

Hailey, when people go from single to being married, they all have different views on how their money will be managed, considered, looked at. Grandpa and I always considered whatever was earned to belong to both of us; it didn't matter who actually brought in the money. We felt we were both working equally for the good of the family. We always made decisions together on how much would be spent and for what. But that is not always the case. My very dear friend Alice's husband, Drew, who worked at a high-paying job, did not think that way. Alice was a stay at home mom, and a wonderful one at that. They had three children; two boys and a girl. She worked really hard making their house a home. She was a great cook and truly the heartbeat of her family. She deeply cared about those in need and wanted to tithe part of their income. Her husband felt differently, and though he was generous to the family, and never denied her what she personally wanted, he insisted on giving a very small weekly donation to the church. She settled for that until he got another huge promotion at work that came with a hefty increase in salary.

On a Saturday night a few months after the pay increase, she mustered up her courage to talk to him about increasing what they gave each week. She talked to him about all the blessings they had been given by God. She reminded him what a good steward our church was. She argued to his sensible business mind that each place the church tithed to was well researched. She virtually pleaded with him that it was her personal desire to be able to give more to help others. But he would not be persuaded. What he gave was still what he wanted to give regardless of his raise.

Drew never hid his feelings that he came to church for his children. From the first time I met him, he was honest about his trouble believing in God. Too many questions his intelligent mind could not resolve. The next morning the family was in their bench as usual. Collection time came. The ushers were going down the pews with the collection basket. Just as one of the ushers, who passed the collection basket every week, was getting to Drew's bench, he was distracted by a loud noise of something that dropped in the back of the church. As he turned to see what it was, his basket actually hit Drew in the head. Hailey, you don't see something like that every day!

The next morning Alice came to see me at the rectory and confidentially told me about the conversation they had had the night before. Granted, what happened could surely be taken by some as a sign that God wanted her husband to give more money in the collection every week. But in my experience, God is never about the money. Her husband had a much greater problem than what he gave in the collection each week. Her husband did not believe God was real!

God speaks to us in personal, intimate ways that we can understand, and that sometimes seem obvious to the people who know us. Drew was intelligent, witty, and had a playful sense of humor that lent itself well to sarcasm. I don't know anyone who appreciated irony more than he did. And what could be more ironic than having just had a conversation with your wife where you refused to give more to church and then the very next day you get hit over the head with the collection basket? I think God chose this most unusual sign to target his particular sense of humor and personality to lovingly show Drew that He was real! But in the end, it was up to Drew to either make the connection that this was a sign from God or to simply dismiss it as just a coincidence, or in his case, and accident.

The Banjo

Hailey, I grew up on books; beloved classics like *The Little Engine That Could, The Emperor's New Clothes, The Little Red Hen, Aesop's Fables, Mother Goose*; too many to mention. The invaluable lessons gleaned from these classics--virtue, wisdom and, just plain fun and silliness--became a part of me. I can't tell you how many times I heard Nana's voice in my head singing that little song, "I think I can, I think I can," as it encouraged me time and time again to never give up. Nana opened the world of books for her children.

But Grandpa's books were music. Pépè Don sounded like Elvis before Elvis did, really, no exaggeration. Mémè Rose played the steel guitar. Musicians came and went all hours of the day and night; and Grandpa and his sister, Linda, learned to sing third and fourth part harmony at a very young age. According to Mémè, Grandpa was singing before he could even talk. Now that might be a little exaggerated. But I do know that as surely as books had entered our souls, music had entered theirs; each of our parents passing on the childhood world that had been gifted to them. In Grandpa's world, there were special musicians who would greatly influence his life, musicians like Jeannine and Red.

Jeannine and Mémè's friendship goes way back to when they were in their 20s still living in the brick blocks. Jeannine played guitar and bass. It was Jeannine who stayed up till the wee hours of the morning playing

Chet Atkins' tunes. Oh, how Grandpa enjoyed listening to and watching those magic fingers. She would also teach him unbelievable chords, licks, and runs. She was his inspiration, and yet, this story is really about her beloved husband, Red.

Like his wife, Red was a musician; classical guitar his first choice. He studied and played so well, and yet, at his first recital he hardly breathed and was so nervous that he said he would never do it again; it just wasn't worth it. His enjoyment turned to sharing his love of music with his wife, quietly playing duets for hours on end.

Red was an individualist, so it seemed fitting when he decided to take up the 5-string banjo. Red fell in love with this old-time instrument, which soon became his life-long passion. He began collecting them and even making his own by hand. He played a rolling banjo and he and Jeannine played in a country band on weekends for years. It would become quite known in New England as Grem Ferris and the Wheels. And on Sundays he played in the folk group at church. It was Red who would later invite Grandpa to join.

It was hard for me to understand how difficult it was for Grandpa to start playing in church, and it was years before he would sing. He could play and sing in clubs and on big stages in front of hundreds of people, but he was nervous to play in church. He explained that the silence, the reverence, the not performing music but praying the music, was the difference. "There is a sacredness to knowing the purpose of why you are there; the music should enhance the liturgy," he'd say. Grandpa fell in love with this music, and was inspired to write scripture- based songs. He wrote a song every week based on the Sunday readings and would teach the arrangements to the group.

Over the years, different musicians came and went, each bringing their own unique talents to the group. For over a decade your mom sang with Grandpa and Jeannine. Someone once commented that it was like hearing a female Brian. But you know, Hailey, your mom joining the folk group was something I never could have foreseen. She would never participate in anything if it meant being in the public eye, never mind singing in front of a full church. It was such a shame because she loved to sing and had a lovely voice. She was invited to join the folk group many times, but always declined. Until this one Sunday morning. When I came out of the sacristy and saw her practicing with the folk group, I couldn't have been more surprised, and confused. I had to laugh when your mother told me how it happened. Believe me when I tell you it wouldn't have happened any other way.

We had just come up from Bible study in the church hall, Grandpa was setting up, and the youth minister asked Jessie if she would do one of the readings for Mass. She wanted to say yes, but anticipating how nervous she'd be, she told her she just couldn't do it. She felt so bad about saying no that she stopped in front of the crucifix, looked at Jesus, and said, "The next thing you ask me to do I promise I'll say yes." A moment later, Jack, the dearest of friends who played acoustic guitar, called Jessie over and asked her if she would sing that morning. Two of the members of the group weren't coming and they needed a good voice! How's that for God's timing?

And truly, those were the glory days; the friendships deepening, the community more and more appreciating the scriptures being sung. The music loved for those beautiful clear sounding banjo notes, and the three-part harmony. It seemed as if it would go on forever. Then one day we got the call that Red had had a massive heart attack; this great and humble man, this true friend, this man of God, died at 57 years old. And the silence of no banjo in church was heard every Sunday.

Red died before Grandpa founded The Lighthouse Coffeehouse. How he would have loved it. Once a month, on a Saturday night, Grandpa and I shared our story and song for the first half of the evening, and Grandpa invited different Christian musicians to share their music for the second half. On the stage, on top of Grandpa's stacked audio system, stood a small lighthouse. It was a replica of Pemaquid Point Light in Maine, with a night-light that shined its steady light to symbolize that Christ was the true Light, sent by God to guide us away from the hidden danger.

On one particular night, we had a guest who brought another musician with him; he played a wonderful acoustic guitar. Grandpa and I were in the audience enjoying their beautiful blend of music, when halfway through their performance the guest musician put his guitar on the stand, opened a case behind him, and pulled out a banjo. This was a surprise; the first and only banjo that was ever played at the Coffeehouse. In the middle of the song, the light on the little lighthouse shut off then went on again. It did this two more times during the song. That was the only banjo tune he played that evening and, when he took up his guitar again, the light stayed lit for the rest of the evening.

When Grandpa packed up the equipment after the night was over, he noticed that the light bulb on the lighthouse was a bit loose. But the fact was, it never reacted during any other song but the banjo tune. There was an eerie feeling in the air when that 5-string banjo began to play and the light went on and off three different times. Grandpa said he played that same rolling style banjo that Red did, and he was sure that Red's spirit had brought the light to his attention. He could see Red smiling, and saying, "I'm here." But you know Grandpa, with all that, he had a hard time believing that it was a sign, even though he had to admit that there couldn't be a better sign in the world for Red to communicate with him. He went back and forth asking himself why God would bother to do something so trivial when people were dying, starving, with so much suffering and violence surrounding us. But he couldn't shake the feeling of Red's spirit being there that night, or feeling his presence so deeply and unmistakably. In the end, Grandpa truly believed that it was a sign from Red that he was there with us in spirit. And it was a sign from God of His love and reality. Grandpa later said something to me that was so simple and yet so profound that I often think of and contemplate his words; "God is the Creator, He doesn't control..."

No Coincidences

After all our years of studying the Bible together, I don't think I have to tell you how serious I am as a teacher. And perhaps a bit controlling. Okay, Hailey, maybe very controlling.

When Grandpa and I first started teaching a mini-series course for 9th graders, I had some real concerns. I wasn't as worried about how serious I am, because I knew Grandpa's unique sense of humor was the perfect complement to lighten things up, and the kids would love him. And they did. I was more worried about my personality. I could already foresee how I would drive myself crazy thinking of such things as, why did I call on that student so much? Did I favor one over the other? How do I pick someone without slighting someone else? Etc., etc. Sometimes there are things about yourself that are impossible to change. However, with a little strategy and a lot of prayer for insight, you can find ways to compensate for your shortcomings. The idea I came up with was to find a way to put God in charge.

It worked out beautifully. We started the class by asking our students to write their names on a piece of paper. We put all the names in a bowl. No matter what we did, whether it was asking a difficult question after a teaching, or one of Grandpa's songs, or choosing parts for a play, anything, I would simply pull a name from the bowl. That way, it was God asking the student the question, not I. It didn't take long to feel that God seemed to know exactly who to ask and when. To make the class more interesting and add some incentive for answering the question correctly, each time they got the answer right they earned one point. I also had previously marked some questions as a bonus. If their name was pulled for that particular question, they got to bet one, two or three points. This was fun and let them know how much they had been paying attention, or not paying attention. If they got the answer wrong they would subtract the points they wagered. We also did many interesting exercises where one person could earn points for their whole table, like the fun jeopardy game we ended with that included all the material that had been covered. At the end of the class we tallied the points. The student with the most points got to choose from a table of assorted prizes, including a hand-made oak walking stick Grandpa had made during the year. We also had a second drawing where a name was pulled from the bowl, which gave everyone an equal chance to win.

One of our activities was reading the Book of Jonah and acting it out as a play. There was a girl in one of our classes named Carinne. I liked her immediately; her excitement and energy, and the fact that she gave it so completely without a thought to what any one else would think. When she found out about the play she jumped up and down and begged to play the part of Jonah. The whole class wanted her to have the part, but I held firm to our decision to put God in charge of everything we did.

Accordingly, we sat in a circle on cushions on the floor with our bowl in the middle and prayed that God would guide our class and give each student the part he/she needed to play to know Him better. There were fourteen students in the class that year. The night before I had written 14 parts on slips of paper-- sailors, the narrator, God, the people of Nineveh, the King, even the fish, for which we had a huge whale for a prop. The person sitting on my left pulled out a slip of paper, unfolded it and read, "sailor." Everyone breathed a sigh of relief. The next student pulled out the part of the Narrator. Each time we made it one closer to Carinne, relief swept the room. She was sitting about eight seats from me in the circle. When it was her turn to reach into the bowl it seemed no one breathed. She closed her eyes, dramatically swished the papers around, grabbed one out and unfolded her paper. When she jumped up and began to scream as the whole class looked on in amazement, there was no doubt she had picked the part of Jonah.

By the end of the course I had fallen in love with all the students. There is such a closeness you feel with them, especially when you are sharing something as incredulous as their faith, the scriptures, and their relationship with Jesus. As a little parting gift, I wanted to write something special to each of them. I decided to look up the meaning of their names and was surprised to see how easy it was to make a connection to that meaning and something I had felt about them during our time together. But I was more than amazed when I saw the meaning of the name Carinne, and couldn't wait to share it with them.

The last night of class, we gathered again on the cushions and I handed each of them a rolled letter that looked like a scroll and was tied with brown twine. I told them how I had looked up the meaning of their names, and truly had felt like their name had been chosen before they were even born. "But," I said, "I think all of you will be particularly interested in knowing the meaning of Carinne." They all crowded around her as she untied the twine and opened her letter for everyone to see. "Carinne. The name Carinne means to keel over, to overturn, or to capsize as in a boat."

It was a miraculous moment; one none of us could have made happen. To think, Hailey, out of 14 students

Carinne had drawn the part of Jonah. I had been moved to write something connected to their name, and in doing so discovered that Carinne actually meant to overturn in a boat. We had put God in charge and in return He had shown us a God who was so near to us, so connected to our lives. A God who can send a sign to tell us He had been right there in the classroom with us all along!

Truly, that experience bonded us together. Whenever we saw Carinne, she would immediately come over and start talking a mile a minute. The years flew by and suddenly she went off to college.

One day, we received a call from a dear friend telling us the shocking news that Carinne had died. She was 27 years old. To me, she would always live on as that eager 9th grader jumping up and down, so excited about her faith.

Hailey, you know that Grandpa faithfully does his readings during the early hours of the morning, usually between 1:00 and 3:00 a.m. He reads from both the Old Testament and the New Testament for about an hour. Each night he follows from where he left off the night before. For over 30 years he has never missed a reading for any reason. The same night we learned of Carinne's death Grandpa got up to do his nightly readings as usual when suddenly I heard him calling me. He wanted me to see that his reading for that night was the Book of Jonah. And God was there!

CHAPTER 5

GOD WORKS IN MYSTERIOUS WAYS

Hailey, there is definitely a student grapevine. As word got out about the prizes we offered at the end of our class, students came determined to win. While the students loved the selection of prizes we offered, Grandpa's walking sticks had soon become the most sought after prize of all. It was wonderful and worth all the work it took to make those precious "sticks." By then, a rolled up scroll burnt around the edges was attached to the stick. Written on the scroll was this explanation Grandpa had carefully prepared to share with the student who won:

It's Not Just A Stick!

The staff or walking stick had its origin in the Bible. When God turned Moses' staff into a snake, it showed that God had given him great power through the staff. Once the staff was linked to the power of God, all the heads of the twelve tribes of Israel wanted their own individual staff of distinct design. (Staffs were different from shepherd's rods, which had a hook at the end of it.) In time common people carried staffs that stood for their family crest; each family publicly identified by the staff they held. Today, we use the staff to represent the spiritual journey we all must take. The staff is used to enhance the spirituality and prayer needed to intentionally put ourselves in God's presence through meditation, for example, such as walking through the woods with this holy symbol.

On a more personal note, these walking staffs are cut from a single tree at just the right time of year, when the sap stops running and the tree becomes dormant for the winter. It is at that time the tree is cut, then left to dry in a holding room for one full year before the staff is debarked and handcrafted to a smooth finish, and the leather strap is added to ensure a better holding grip. Much time and respect for the wood is given to each staff. Enjoy it and may God bless the one who carries it on their journey.

Brian and Phyllis Calvey, the Lighthouse Ministry

My greatest memory of the walking stick happened between two cousins who attended one of our Lighthouse Confirmation programs at another parish, one year apart. The first cousin won the walking stick the year he attended. When the second cousin attended our retreat a year later, he walked in determined that he would win the walking stick too. Unbeknown to us, the mothers of the boys had had a big falling out and neither the boys nor their families had spoken to each other in over three years. When the second cousin won the walking stick both boys took it as a sign that Jesus wanted them to forgive each other. Their feelings were so strong about this that when they told their mothers how they felt the families actually made amends. It was a great healing not only for their two families but for the parish as well. When the story was told to us, I felt a chill go through me. Though the retreats focus so much on Jesus' teaching that God will forgive us as we forgive others, only the two of them could have made the connection that both of them winning the walking sticks was a sign that was sent from God. Signs, indeed, are such intimate conversations between God and us.

5:14

I never would have believed how much I loved teaching 9th and 10th graders. And Hailey, they never would have believed how much they affected our lives.

One year we had a student in our class named Travis who reminded me of your Uncle Trevor in a lot of ways; he was quiet, intelligent, and serious.

The second week of class, we sat on cushions in a circle and he stretched his long legs out on the floor, feet crossed with his construction boots resting on each other. The "bowl" chose him to read the story of Jonah aloud to the class. When he finished reading, I was taken aback when he couldn't stop himself from saying how he didn't blame Jonah a bit for being angry. "Three days and all's forgiven. No way!" he said. "These people did wrong and they need to pay for it. Other wise it just wasn't fair." He was so emotional in his argument that he soon had persuaded the rest of the class that God should definitely punish those people despite their willingness to repent. There was a feeling of righteous revenge in the air.

That week had started out very busy for Grandpa and me. Monday night we went to the prison. We had been going for years. It was such a joy to be part of the Bethany community at MCI Norfolk. Once a month, after their Monday Mass, which was their Sunday celebration, we did a prayer service using our Lighthouse story and song format. The men knew that my birthday was on Thursday and, for a special surprise, they commissioned an artist in prison to draw a picture for me; a breathtaking scene of a lighthouse with gorgeous flowers growing all around. But what brought tears to my eyes was the lighthouse beam that was shining forth in the form of a cross. The picture was in the center of a huge poster board. Over the pretty pastel drawing were the words, "Many blessings on this your birthday." On the inside of the card on the left-hand side, in carefully hand-drawn orange writing, were the words from Matthew's Gospel, "You are like light for the whole world. A city built on a hill cannot be hid. No one lights a lamp and puts it under a bowl; instead he puts it on the lamp stand, where it gives light for everyone in the house. In the same way your light must shine before people, so that they will see the good things you do and praise your Father in heaven." (Matthew 5:14-16). And on the right side and the back of the card were the signatures and birthday wishes from all the men. Sr. Ruth told me it took a month for the men to complete this treasured gift to me.

The card was in the living room and, for no particular reason except that I would be teaching on my birthday, I grabbed it on our way out the door when we left for our mini series course. If it worked out to use it, I would share it with the class. In any case, I was really pleased we would be spending my birthday doing God's work in this special way.

After Travis' surprising reaction to the story of Jonah, it was time for a break. We sat around four long tables made up in a square, eating the chocolate double fudge brownies I had made for a snack. The card was leaning on the wall in the room and I casually picked it up and placed it on the table. "Today is my birthday," I began, "May 14, and I wanted to share this card the men at Norfolk prison gave me on Monday." I explained about our prison ministry. They were very interested and had lots of questions. We talked about what it felt like to go through the trap. Not to be able to take anything with you. And to hear the door shut behind you as you walked into the yard. They looked at the card and seemed surprised that such a talented artist would be in prison. I held up the card and opened it, pointing out the quote on the Bible verse written so plainly on the bottom of the card: Matthew 5:14. Still, they didn't make the connection. "You should have seen the men's faces that night when I pointed to the quote they had picked for my birthday," I explained. "You see, my birthday is today, and with all the verses to choose from, the men picked a verse that was the actual date of my birthday, May 14th – 5:14, and they never even realized it until I showed it to them." The kids looked as surprised as the men did when I pointed it out to them, but now they got it. "Can you believe it?" I asked. They were impressed, and still so interested that I ventured on.

"The men all have a story to tell," I continued. "I remember going to the prison one Father's Day weekend and chose the theme of fathers for our presentation. I told them stories about the Sunday baseball games we had on our big front lawn and how my father would invite any neighborhood kids that looked eager to play to join us. I told them about the pig piles and pillow fights. And after several more stories about my own father, I asked them to say one word that reminded them of a memory of their father. A young man, who looked no older than 19, raised his hand. When I nodded to him he said, "heating grate." I thought I had heard wrong but he continued. "We were seven boys in our family," he said, "and we were always in trouble. Tough kids in a tough neighborhood, and we boys had made a reputation for ourselves. But whenever we did anything wrong and it got back to my father, he would make us kneel for the whole afternoon on the heating grate that was on the kitchen floor. After you couldn't stand the pain anymore you'd dare to shift the weight off your knees and in return get a good backhand in the head. Sometimes he'd take the stick off the wall and would hit us in the back and tell us to straighten up. He said that would make us think twice about getting into trouble again.

"I did more stuff and ended up in here. I was bitter and angry, and knew my behavior just made it worse but I just didn't care. Then the guy in my cell asked me to come to the chapel on Monday night. I said we never went to church when we was kids. My father didn't believe in nothin' like that. But he wouldn't give up. He kept talking to me till finally I agreed to come and just try it out." He put his head down and shook it for a moment as if remembering. "I couldn't believe what I was hearing about God, that He was a loving Father who loved His children unconditionally." His voice choked. "A God of mercy and forgiveness. I never knew a father like that." He stopped talking as tears sprang into his eyes. The man next to him put his hand on his shoulder. "It's alright," he encouraged, "you're with friends here." "Coming here changed my life," he continued. "I even think I'll be able to forgive my own father one day."

I told a few more stories. The illiteracy. The drugs. Mental illness. Foster homes. Alcoholism. Abuse. And about a 10-year-old boy who had run away to join the circus. They were glued to every word. "Of course they've done things that are very wrong," I said. "And they are paying the consequences society demands, and rightly so. But with all the love I've been given in my life, I don't want to be the one to judge them, or to say that God should not forgive them when they are sorry and ask for forgiveness." You could hear a pin drop. I laid the card down and watched their faces soften as they read the handwritten messages. "You have touched us all with your love." "No one needs love more than someone who doesn't deserve it."

It was a quiet walk back to the classroom. When the parts were picked for the play, Travis drew the part of God. And as convincing as he had been to stir the class's emotion to punishment, he now played the part of God with such a spirit of forgiveness that he made the author of the Book of Jonah proud. Jonah, chosen because it means dove; the sign in both the Old and New Testaments of a time for a new beginning, a time for God's forgiveness.

At the end of the class Travis had the most points and couldn't decide if he wanted the oak-staff or the Jesus and the Lighthouse picture that Grandpa had beautifully sketched. I was surprised when he finally decided on the picture. Being the winner, he got to pull the name for the second prize. At that point I always reminded the students that there was no such thing as coincidence with God. Even in this small way God could communicate with us. And Hailey, every year there was no doubt to me or to the class why God chose the person for that second prize, which greatly affected not only the one receiving it, but all of us. Travis reached in the bowl and pulled out his own name! It was the only time in all our years of teaching that the same person had ever won both prizes. He was ecstatic and immediately went for the staff. After the drawing, no one seemed to want to leave. We sat in the circle and Travis was sitting opposite me. I felt him wanting to say something. He hesitated, but after a while caught my eye and said, "My birthday is May 14th too!"

"18 and Life"

When Trevor was in the 3rd grade he wrote a story called "A Day in Our Garden." What really impressed me was that he had written the story in the third person. It began simply: "Trevor got up on a Saturday morning, and it was a day to work with the family in the garden." As I continued to read, it made me happy to see how he described each chore with such detail, even the way Grandpa methodically rolled and unrolled the garden hose. Sometimes you just don't think your kids are paying that much attention! But it was the ending that really caught me by surprise, and I laughed out loud as I read what he had written: "When they worked in the garden, Trevor's mother would always ask him to wear his farmer overalls, his work boots, and his garden hat. Because when Trevor wore those clothes he always seemed to work better." You know, Hailey, until I read those words I never even realized I asked him to do that. But the truth was, the clothes he wore did make him feel differently. The old adage was true: clothes make the man. There was no getting around it, those clothes seemed to make him feel like a farmer, and he really did work harder when he had them on.

When Trevor was a teenager you wouldn't have recognized your uncle, who is always dressed so smart looking now. Back in those days the sight of his clothes made me break into a cold sweat. He wore jeans that he sliced at the knees, and convinced Mémè to sew the holes with red bandanas. His rock t-shirts sent chills up my spine, and I've since tried to erase them from my memory. He tied a bandana around his should-length curly blonde hair, and to complete the mood he wore tall, black, combat boots. Bet you can't believe I would allow that, uh? But regardless of the clothes he wore, I always saw that good little boy who worked with us in the garden; kind, softhearted and helpful. And he wore better clothes to school and dressed appropriately for church. At home, though, his clothes seemed to be the perfect match for the music that blasted from his room, music that marked a course for rebellion against any form of authority.

Trevor's room was the one Caleb has now, and with the open A-frame house there was no place for me to escape the loud music. It was Saturday, Grandpa was working, and your mom was at a friend's house. I had just come in with the morning mail. Our church envelopes had arrived and, even though I had written the tithing letter myself, it was still a welcome sight. In each mailing I wrote a letter to the parishioners explaining how our parish was reaching out to those in need. As I sat in the rocking chair to read the letter again, I tried my best to block out the music. Suddenly, Trevor broke my concentration as he yelled down to me, "Listen to this song."

It was an unspoken agreement between us. I listened to his things and he listened to mine. He put the music on pause and automatically brought down the words so I could follow along. I could never seem to make the words out through all the screaming and loud playing, and it often surprised me how much I appreciated the lyrics.

Trevor played a song by Skid Row called "18 and Life." I read along and slowly found myself entering the violent, inner-city world of a teenager, who from birth never had a chance in life. Alcohol, abuse, despair, a gun, no one to care, and now, at eighteen this young boy faced a life sentence in prison.

When the song was over, Trevor turned off the music. "Why bother?" he asked in despair. "Your generation has ruined the world. Look at the mess we're in, all this violence and crime, kids who don't have a chance in life. And it's too late, it's gotten too big for anyone to stop it." His eyes mirrored the music that he listened to over and over again, and he seemed caught in its relentless down beat.

Instead of commenting about the song, I asked Trevor to read the tithing letter I still had in my hands. I could not believe the timing, the perfect timing of getting this letter at this exact moment. Since 1984 our church had tithed to many places and for many purposes. But never before to a center that dealt specifically with young boys who could no longer live at home because of family circumstances. Never, that is, until now.

He took the letter up to his room and read about our community's latest outreach -- $3,000.00 which would be matched by the State to fund a newly opening Community Mental Health Center in Rhode Island. This facility would house young boys from 16 to 20 who were living in such terrible situations that they could no longer stay at home. Somehow, those words seemed too mild to reflect what that really meant. Counseling and training for independent living would be provided. Through this program, these young people would live in a setting of loving relationships, and have role models, which had been sorely missing in their lives. This would give them a chance in life to cross over to a new way of living; it would change the whole direction of their lives. Our donation would provide the furniture, dishes, etc. to furnish their new living quarters.

Trevor didn't comment about the letter but it was enough for me that he read it and knew that as a community we were doing something to effect change. In a very real way, we were trying to prevent these boys from being the next "18 and Life."

It was many years later that I asked Trevor if he would consider coming to the prison with us on a Monday night. I had told the men many stories about him, and they had recently asked if Trevor would ever consider coming in so they could meet him. Trevor was always interested to hear about their lives, and Grandpa and I often shared stories with him that the men were comfortable with us sharing. Trevor really wanted to go but said he was not good at sharing his feelings or speaking in a crowd. "Exactly what would I have to do?" he asked in a very concerned voice.

"Just sit with us," I told him. "Dad will sing and I'll tell a few stories and you won't even have to say anything unless you want to. They really just want to meet you," I assured him. "I'll think about it and let you know when I make my decision," he answered. "By the way, next month I'm planning a theme about your trying years," I said with a sparkle in my eyes. "I wonder if you'd mind if I told them the story about the day you were up in your room and played that song for me by Skid Row. Do you remember the name of it?" He answered without hesitation, "18 and Life. But that was a popular song when I was a teenager. I haven't heard them play it on the radio now in years. Do you think the men will even know it?"

"Well, that doesn't really matter. I already planned on explaining what the song was about for those who had never heard it. Anyway, it's what happened that day that I really want to share. Do you remember?"

"Yeah," he mumbled, but the look in his eyes told me that the whole incident was instantly replaying in that incredible memory of his. "I still can't get over how that tithing letter arrived just at that moment when we were discussing kids who never had a chance in life," I continued. "Now, don't tell me you don't believe that God arranges those moments to speak to us in some way?" I asked. He gave me one of those looks. "Regardless, do you think that will be a good story to share with the men?" He thought for a moment. "Well, I'll bet they will certainly be able to relate to it," he answered in his logical manner.

"You know Trev, you wouldn't believe how often the men start sharing by saying, "Well, we could all tell our stories of abuse, but..." It's just a fact of life for most of them. I can't even imagine." We were still talking about the men's lives when a car pulled in the driveway. "You know dad has rehearsal at the house tonight," I said. "Would you want to go and visit Nana and Pépè with me?" Frankly, Hailey, even though he liked to visit them, I was surprised he agreed. I couldn't often get him to do things like that anymore. We continued to talk about the prison all the way over, and then spent a wonderful evening with Nana and Pépè.

As we got into the van to go home, Trevor turned on the radio and immediately switched it to his station. His head turned toward me so quickly that I was startled, and by the look on his face, I thought something terrible had happened. "Do you know what song is playing?" he asked incredulously. I listened, but didn't recognize the song. "It's 18 and Life," he said, still almost refusing to believe it. My heart started pounding as he held my gaze with those intent blue eyes of his. "They just don't play that song on the radio any more. They haven't played it in years." He shook his head, reading my mind without my having to say a word.

In fact, neither of us spoke another word. We listened intently to the rest of the song and when it was over, he did something he never ever did. He shut off the radio. It seemed impossible to listen to another sound when God had become so real, right there in our Caravan. It was an intimate moment between us, and I know Trevor made his decision right then and there to come to the prison.

And he did come to the prison with us the following month. The men were so excited. When he walked through the door of the chapel they stood up and applauded, greeting him as if a celebrity had just walked in. He was a little taken back by that, but so were Grandpa and I. They all rushed to greet him. One young man in his early 20's kiddingly tapped his arm and said, "Hey, you don't look like the type of kid who'd kick the wall!"

After liturgy, Grandpa and I took our usual places and Trevor sat with us facing the men. Grandpa sang one song and I told a story, but it was so obvious that the men wanted to talk that I stopped and asked if anyone had anything to share. When they all seemed to be focused on Trevor, he gave me a look that said, "You told me I wouldn't have to say anything." But it was too late for that now. Two of the men sitting in the last bench looked at Trevor and said, "We've been waiting a long time to ask you one question." I could see Trevor's back tense up. "Is that okay with you?" they asked. He said yes so they continued. "We just want to know one thing. Are the stories your mother tells really true?"

Trevor grinned at me, and for a minute I wasn't sure what he was going to say. He loved doing that. "Yes," he finally answered, "the stories are all true." "When did you know you had something special going?" someone asked. "Did you realize things were different in your family?" another wanted to know. The questions poured out. Trevor answered them all and even seemed to relax. I loved hearing that logical, intelligent mind of his sharing with the men who had become our brothers in Christ. I was so proud of him. But I must say it surprised both Grandpa and me when he shared that sometimes it was difficult having parents who loved you so much. Some of his friends had parents who didn't seem to care what they did, and it made life much easier for them. They just did what they wanted. On the other hand, everything seemed to matter to us. And everything he did seemed to affect our lives.

As I sat and listened to Trevor and the men dialogue, it suddenly dawned on me that if I had shared stories of abuse they would not have questioned the truth of it for even a second. But stories of a loving family who were there for each other; this they couldn't quite believe. Porch lights that were never shut off until you came home, even if it was in the early hours of the morning. I didn't realize until Trevor came that night that all my "bad stories" sounded like good stories to them. To a parent, a bad story was sharing the pain and worry of lying in bed most of the night half awake, praying, listening for the sound of familiar tires turning into the crushed stone driveway.

From their perspective it was a good story; a teenager was coming home in the early hours of the morning and a parent couldn't sleep until he was safely home. From that night on the stories I told in the prison chapel would always sound different to me. Then something happened for which I was not prepared. The men began to share their personal stories; private, quiet men, who had never before spoken in the group.

"Trevor," one man began, "My mother left us when I was seven and my father took to drinking even more after that. I guess he tried to do his best by us, but after my mother left things were never the same. I got in with a wild crowd and started drinking every chance I got. This one night I was on my way out with my friends and my father begged me not to go. But I had stopped listening long ago. Well, we all went to this bar and things got way out of control. The last thing I remember was waking up on the floor with a knife in my hand. I honestly don't recall what happened. Do you know how many times in the last ten years I've replayed that one moment over and over again, wishing I would have listened to my father? I can't take it back. I can't change what happened. Listen to your parents, Trev, they only want what's best for you."

Trevor nodded his head and smiled at the man. "I guess we all have similar stories to tell," another man started. "And believe me none of us are excusing our behavior. Let's face it, we made the wrong choices and we're here as punishment for what we did. What got me here was what basically gets most of us here, drugs and alcohol. I started drinking when I was twelve. My mother raised us alone. We lived in a kind of ghetto, and my poor mother would have cried to see me so many mornings waking up in those gutters. There was so much violence and street gangs. One night there was a fight and I shot someone in self defense, but it didn't come out that way in the trial. I was 21 when that happened, Trevor. A young, rebellious kid angry at the world." His sad eyes were so remorseful. "That was 25 years ago. Don't you think I've changed? No one is more aware than me that I can't bring that kid back to life, but at some point I'd like to know I've been forgiven. We've become new men in this chapel. For the first time we know what it's like to have Jesus in our life to guide us. You have all that. Don't let drinking and making the wrong choices rob you of everything in life that means anything. I broke my mother's heart, and I couldn't even go to her funeral when she died two years ago."

Trevor was visibly moved by their testimonies. It took all of my will power to hold back the tears. They knew how deeply I loved my son and prayed every day that he would be guided to make the right decisions and stay away from the drinking trap that many of his close friends had fallen into. One mistake, one moment of careless driving, could take a life, could take his life. I looked at these men, many of them young enough to be my own son. Then I suddenly understood what was happening. This was their gift to me, sharing their story in hopes that what happened to them might influence Trevor's life decisions in some positive way. For now, it was all they had to give.

"18 and Life." A song from Trevor's past; the sign God chose to invite him to go to the prison with us where he would meet many men who were living the very words to a song that had affected him so much during his teenage years. That night, in the most dramatic way possible, God told Trevor exactly what He wanted him to hear. And the best part

of the story, Hailey, is that Trevor was listening...

CHAPTER 6

GOD'S SUDDEN INTENTIONAL

PRESENCE!

The Red Cardinal

It was the week before Christmas and I did not want to go to Bible study that Sunday morning. Hailey, we had been studying Luke's gospel for some time now, and were just coming to the scene of the crucifixion. Being in the midst of all the preparations to celebrate His birth, I could not bear to read the account of His death. Nevertheless, the four of us went as usual; your mother, Trevor, Grandpa and I. To my relief I found the Pastor must have felt the same way as I did. When we opened our Bibles to where we had left off the previous week, he asked us to turn instead to the account of Jesus' birth. After we finished reading the well-known story where Mary laid the baby in a manger because there was no room for them in the inn, there was the usual pause to give us all a moment to reflect. A rather shy woman, who had just recently joined our Bible group, got up the courage to ask a question. "I grew up in the city, and I feel stupid for asking this," she apologized, "but I don't know what a manger is. What exactly is a manger anyway?" she repeated.

Hailey, when I was growing up I went to our barn every night with my father to feed the horses, and would soon learn that I didn't know any more than she did what a manger was. Whenever I heard that word, the only picture that came to mind was the same one that always came to mind - the manger depicted in the holy cards – what seemed to me to be a handmade little brown bed with wooden crosspieces and filled with golden straw to make the bed soft. I pictured it in the middle of a barn with heavenly rays streaming down illuminating this little baby. What an awakening to learn that morning that the manger was not a bed at all – it held food! The manger was a feeding trough; the place where animals came to eat. My mind began to reel with this new information. The manger was about food. Food! The first food God sent from heaven to feed God's people was manna. Now Jesus was being sent from heaven by God and was placed in a manger. Luke said the manger shall be the sign to look for. What was Luke bringing to our attention by calling the manger a sign to look for? I remembered the prophet Isaiah using the manger as a warning to God's people that they would not know where their food was. The pieces kept coming.

By the next morning I was so excited that instead of working on the book I was writing at the time, I put it aside to write down all that had happened at Bible study that Sunday. I took out my pen and a new notebook. Can you believe it, Hailey, no computer at that time? It was the timing of what happened next that startled me. At the precise moment I pressed my pen to paper to write that first word, a red cardinal made his sudden, noisy, appearance from seemingly out of nowhere, landing on the feeder right outside my window. The perfect timing was connected with an undeniable feeling of God's sudden intentional presence. The sign felt like God was telling me to continue writing what I was learning and experiencing that pertained to Him. And as I continued to do so, God affirmed this feeling by communicating with me through the sign of the cardinal.

The stories I wrote during that time period were eventually and surprisingly published. I say, surprisingly because, as your Uncle Trevor would so honestly say when I sent the manuscript out, "mom, I don't want to hurt your feelings, and I love your stories, but nobodys don't get published." It seemed almost a miracle that the first publishing company I sent it to accepted the book. I was elated when my editor helped me formulate an outline for a second book.

All was going well until my third project, which included many years of working on a series of books. There were some snags, and just when it seemed like everyone was finally on board, my editor, who had by then become a good friend, reluctantly called to tell me a decision had been made to cancel the project. As I stood with phone in hand, staring out the window trying to grasp the explanation of it all, a red cardinal suddenly landed on a branch in the green fir tree. I walked quickly over to the window, subconsciously, I think, testing him to fly away. A cardinal is a very skittish bird, and by right should have flown away immediately. However, my steps toward him did not affect him in the least. In fact, he never budged from that branch during the entire heartbreaking conversation. It was the strangest feeling; like being in a fog, half listening to what my editor was saying, while mesmerized by the tuft of feathers on the cardinal's head softly blowing in the cold wind as that bird continued to look straight at me. The sign of the cardinal had been connected to God's communication for so long, that seeing it at that critical time, gave me the strength to immediately trust in God's will. Even before we hung up, I knew in my heart that God was telling me that this, too, was part of His Plan. Whenever I needed to feel that assurance again, I closed my eyes and could see, as I can even now, the tuft of feathers on the cardinal's head blowing in the cold wind. While sometimes I've found that the echo of words can fade, the gift of a sign is unforgettable.

The Horseshoe

Oh Hailey, you would have loved our horses, and our barn, as makeshift as it was. Time meant something different in a barn. Something made you move quietly and slowly; perhaps so you could hear the barn sounds, from the crackling of leather to the soft neighing of the horses. The horses always warmed the barn for us, and I learned so many lessons inside that warm place. After my chores were done, I would sit for a while on that old wood plank floor, my back resting on the wall, dreaming, listening to my father patiently brushing Sarachanna, one of our sweet mares, in her stall.

One year, our Pastor invited me to give the Thanksgiving reflection of the Gospel, which was the parable of the rich man who wanted to pull down his barns to build greater ones. I knew immediately what story I wanted to use, but it centered on a colt that was born in our barn, and was very different from the stories I usually told in church. For that reason, I continued to go back and forth with another story that was more traditional.

It was only a week until Thanksgiving and I still couldn't decide which to choose. That Sunday the four of us, your mom, Trevor, Grandpa and I, took our usual long hike in our back woods. We all got our walking sticks off their pegs on the wall and started up the first big, steep, rocky hill. As we carefully made our way up, I couldn't believe my eyes. There, nearly buried in the loose gravel, with only one corner barely sticking out of the ground, was a horseshoe! In our many years of walking, from the time we built our A-frame house when your mom was only three, we'd seen many horses on the paths, in the sandpit, and on the pipeline. But never once did we ever find or see a horseshoe. And believe me I would have remembered and brought it home as a good luck piece to hang over our shed door, which I did immediately with this one. I was overjoyed that God had used a sign to speak to me again; my decision was clearly made!

In the middle of telling that story on Thanksgiving morning, my attention was drawn to a young mother, a dear friend of mine in one of our evening Bible groups, who began sobbing uncontrollably in her bench. This really took me by surprise because it was so uncharacteristic of her personality. She was always careful to keep her emotions in check, and never one to share about her personal life. Of course all sorts of things started to cross my mind. As soon as our service was over she came to apologize. She hoped that it hadn't been too distracting for me. I wished she would have shared what she was going through, but she would only say that she had come to a serious crossroad in her life and had been praying for what direction to take. When I started telling the story she described feeling as if she slipped into another world, and everyone around her had disappeared. Every word I spoke felt as if God was speaking directly to her through me. All the feelings she had been holding in for so long suddenly broke loose, and when it was over, she came out of the trance-like state, in control of her emotions again, knowing exactly what she was supposed to do. She hugged me and told me that she could never explain how hearing that story had changed her life.

I learned something that day about signs that I had never really given thought to until that happened. The experience opened up a deeper realm of understanding how God acts with so many people in mind. Even though I knew the sign had been necessary for me to choose the story God wanted me to tell that day, I felt the sign wasn't really for me after all, if you know what I mean Hailey. Perhaps that's the reason it sometimes has to take as long as it does for God to answer us: events have to be perfectly in line for everyone involved in the situation. And that's why the signs God sends are always so powerful – each sign is so unique, so personal, and so patiently planned!

The Mother Robin

Hailey, I'm sure you must remember the time Grandpa and I noticed a mother robin starting to build a nest between the ten roof rafters out on our front porch. She started a little pile of building materials, but when she came back she dropped the next bits of twigs in the rafter next to it. Soon she had started a third nest in the rafter next to that one. Grandpa tried knocking down all the nests but one, only to have her begin the others again the next day. Besides being tired of having to clean up the mess she made, we were afraid she'd simply wear herself out. So we put Caleb's wooden snake up on the support beam to try to persuade her to find a better place to build her home. When you discovered the decoy snake up there, Hailey, it didn't take long for you to figure out the reason for it. You made me promise that we wouldn't do anything else to stop her from building her nest there.

The next morning you came to check on everything, and the wooden snake was missing. You asked if we had taken it down. We were surprised it was gone, too, because we hadn't touched it, and then Grandpa spotted it on the ground. We couldn't believe that robin had pushed the decoy snake off that beam, but you just smiled at the two of us, having no doubt about it at all. That robin seemed bound and determined to stay, and that was that. In the end she finally did settle between the last rafters to build her nest; a good sign, as the corner seemed the most secure place.

This was not the first time a robin started to build a nest on our porch. But our door opens too often and, sadly, those precious blue eggs are soon abandoned. There was only one mother robin that did make it and hatched all four eggs. One morning though, shortly afterward, we found a baby bird chirping on the grass. I thought it had accidently fallen from the nest. Grandpa explained to me that if a baby bird is sick the mother instinctively knows and will push the bird from the nest. Not wanting to accept what he was telling me, I insisted he put it back. Within hours the baby bird was kicked out again. We did everything humanly possible to keep it alive, and I remembered all too well how painful it was to watch this little life fight so hard in vain to live. No, not again. You were too young to understand, but I was going through a very hard, painful time just then. And for the first time in my life, I remember closing up, wanting to shut myself away and not allow myself to be open to any kind of hurt again. Even to the point of not wanting this robin to abandon another baby on our doorstep.

But this robin, like you, had a different idea. And suddenly we were all being drawn into her daily activities. I was standing behind the sliding glass door watching her, marveling as she did her final dance, going round and round, cementing the nest with her own God-given glue. Relief of sorts; the first step was accomplished. We continued our watch. When Grandpa sensed the timing was right, he carried out his plan. He placed a high stool on the deck. As soon as we opened the door she flew away as usual. Quickly, Grandpa climbed onto the stool and showed you and Caleb how to use what you aptly named his "spy mirror," the mirror mechanics used to look in places where you can't see directly. Hailey, you screamed out with excitement when it was your turn: "Grandma, there's four blue eggs!" I was the last one to look into the nest. Those four perfect eggs tugged at my heart. She had made it against such odds.

It was soon Mother's Day and my birthday. Hailey, I was born on Mother's Day and my birthday only landed on Mother's Day about every eleven years. When it did, it always felt like an extra special day. Grandpa called you and Caleb to come to the porch. You immediately saw the spy mirror in his hand and without a word each of us took our turn climbing on the stool. The first egg had hatched. By nightfall all four of the babies had broken out of their shells. "Grandma," you whispered to me, "I think God made this happen today as a special present for your birthday." I'll always remember how you leaned your head on my shoulder, and we stood there together silently watching the mother robin keeping her babies warm. All that time, she kept her eye on us but didn't fly away.

Soon little beaks were reaching up over the nest with their mouths open wide calling out for food. Every day I would check to make sure there were still four of them. The two in the front were the biggest. "Come on now, feed that one in the back," I'd say as if the mother could hear me, "she hasn't had her turn in a while." And I would anxiously watch until I could see it had been fed.

In the midst of all the activity, another robin showed up. What was this robin's intention, I wondered? By this time, we all felt so protective of our mother robin. We studied the situation and it seemed as if the other robin was coming to the nest, too; yet, it was hard to be absolutely sure until we saw the two robins at the nest together. What a touching sight. I never realized both robin parents fed their young. They took turns coming and going though the mother robin seemed to make many more trips. Your cousin, Ella, was over one day and had her own explanation. She spent the morning looking out the glass door watching the mother come to feed, and would not take her eyes off the nest until the father came back. Then she would clap her hands.

"Where does he go for so long?" she asked. And before I could answer her, she said, "I know, the dad is at work and comes home every chance he can."

The last week of May, Grandpa spotted the first bird fly off on its own. He showed us the mother close-by chirping encouragement for her babies to come to her. One by one they took their leap of faith. It was breathtaking to watch them build up their courage to leave the safety of that nest.

"There's one of the babies," Grandpa pointed out as we sat on the swing in our yard a few days later. "See the spots they have on their feathers. Those spots will fade away when they get a little older. Look, there's the mother and father," he said. "Notice how they're still teaching them what to do." Each day we searched to find those young birds until one day they blended into adulthood.

Hailey, oftentimes during the days that followed I found myself staring at the empty nest, surprised how lonely I was for each moment it had brought, in spite of the mess, even the worry. Then one morning I looked out the sliding glass door and there were bits of straw, grass, twigs and sticks strewn across our porch. I made a cup of coffee and sat in the rocking chair watching the new robin fly back and forth depositing materials in three different rafters. I felt as happy as Ella, wanting to clap my hands with delight. And that's when it struck me. There was no thought to try to control or change anything. Suddenly it didn't seem to matter about the mess; I was ready for what lie ahead. God had been trying to talk to me about opening up again, learning to get past the hurt and pain and move forward. Yet, I continued to chase His conversation away. So He sent a sign that simply wouldn't be chased away. And through this sign I finally heard all that God wanted to say.

CHAPTER 7

Achieving flight!

O *ne day a man was watching a butterfly try to break free from its cocoon. He watched the butterfly struggle and then it seemed to stop, as if it could go no further. Hoping to ease the butterfly's situation, the man took a pair of scissors and snipped off the remaining bit of the cocoon. The butterfly then emerged easily but its wings were all shriveled. The man waited, expecting the wings to soon expand but nothing happened. The butterfly spent its life crawling around and was never able to fly. What the man did not understand was that the struggle to break free from its cocoon, forcing fluid from its body into its wings, was crucial for the butterfly's development. Flight could only be achieved in that way...*

Bob Returns Home

Hailey, I knew Bob was planning to return home on Labor Day weekend. And you know me, Hailey, I wanted to call him right away, but I forced myself to wait a few weeks to give him a chance to settle back in. However, he ended up coming home a few weeks earlier than he had anticipated. By the time I called, he was in the middle of renovating his kitchen, a project that was planned before they left. He laughed when he told me about the mess they were living in, and I tried hard not to sound too anxious to meet with him. Before we hung up, he had insisted it would be no trouble if your mom and I went to visit him the following Friday.

His directions were great and soon we were trying to find a place to park as his double driveway was filled with work trucks. The house was a friendly garrison, warmly decorated, and welcoming. When we walked up the stairs and onto the front porch, the foreman stuck his head out of the protective heavy plastic sheets that were hanging across the now open room to contain the dust to the kitchen area. He was on the watch for us, and said Bob would be here in a few minutes. Meanwhile, Bob had set up a comfortable place in the breezeway for us to talk. As Jessie and I waited for him to return, I looked at the bookcase-like shelving in front of us filled with canned goods and kitchen supplies; every space in that small room packed from floor to ceiling. The whole busy, friendly setting seemed to tell the story of their life; other people's needs first, always comings and goings, and lots of activity. Bob came rushing in apologizing for being late; he had been called to make an unexpected donor run to the hospital that was time sensitive.

Hailey, if you could meet kindness, that's what it would be like meeting Bob. With one hug you knew he was a friend, open and caring, concerned for you and not for himself. After quickly touching base with the carpenters, he came and sat in the chair opposite the two-seated couch Jessie and I were sitting on. Behind him was a sliding glass door that led to the backyard and allowed sunshine to stream in and heat the somewhat chilly room. He crossed his long leg over his knee, smiled, and asked me what I wanted to know exactly. I explained how his words to Jackie and Madonna the night of John Paul's wake, "welcome to the butterfly club," had intrigued me and I wanted to find out more about it. But first, I wanted to hear about his daughter and her brave fight in her battle with leukemia. When he spoke that precious name out loud, AnneMarie, he immediately broke down, and we soon decided it might be easier if he told us stories as they came to mind. I've written down what I think is a pretty accurate account of what he shared with us that day.

It is interesting how butterflies first came into his life; and how they became the way he told AnneMarie how much she meant to him and how they'd be in the fight together. After relapsing, AnneMarie had to move on to another hospital so she could have a bone marrow transplant in hopes of saving her life. It was difficult leaving Hasbro Children's Hospital, a place where they had warm feelings because of the treatment they received there. It was like starting all over again, and it was scary. Someone who had gone through it before had alerted them to BMT support online. (The mission of the Bone Marrow Transplant Support Group is to uphold those who suffer the effects of illness before, during and after a bone marrow transplant). While exploring, Bob told us they read a story by Kendra Marsh, a bone marrow transplant recipient, called "Freeing the Monarch." Kendra's transplant nurse had given her a gift – a beautiful butterfly snow-globe, and she accidentally dropped it. Instead of being devastated by what had happened, she saw the butterfly as being "free," and in that moment she felt she also was finally free of her own cancer battle. The story was so encouraging and inspiring to Bob that he hurried out and bought AnneMarie the most beautiful musical snow-globe he could find – with two butterflies inside. He gave it to her with a note that expressed many things but mainly stated that there were two butterflies trapped in the glass because she'd never be in this alone, that they'd fight together until they were both free from leukemia's clutches.

Being in that room that morning felt like we had been given a small space in time where the four of us, your mother, me, Bob and AnneMarie, were in that butterfly snow-globe, safely tucked inside a smaller world apart from the world, and yet somehow still a part of it. Bob would tell a story, which would remind him of another story, and as he held us captive with each one, we all took turns crying. My tears first came when Bob described sitting by AnneMarie's bedside as she asked questions like, "Will I lose my hair?" "Is there truly an afterlife?" And the unspoken question Bob saw in her eyes, "Will I die?" It was emotional hearing Bob describe the pain he felt as he watched the tears spring up in AnneMarie's eyes, knowing how helpless they both were to change things. It was all the more emotional sitting near my own sweet daughter, when just the thought of having to say goodbye to her was unimaginable. Hailey, as he spoke about AnneMarie asking those questions, for one second my mind drifted back to a night when your mother and I had talked till the early hours of the morning. Though it didn't seem like the right time then to talk about our own lives, I do want to share that night with you now.

It was early November. The leaves had fallen. It had been chilly enough earlier to light a fire in the wood stove, but by nighttime the house was so warm we had the sliding door opened, relishing the late autumn breeze that floated in. Trevor and Grandpa had gone to bed, and Jessie and I were still sitting on the couch talking at one o'clock in the morning. It was the strangest feeling. Sometimes I felt like the mother looking at my daughter, and yet the conversations were so much like the ones I'd had with my own mother that, at times, I slipped back into feeling like the daughter, sitting across from my own mother again.

There was no rhyme or reason to the conversation. Jessie had just started her first year of college, and her courses – such as child development and women's psychology – supplied endless questions that just came into her head, and we would talk about them. Sometimes her questions surprised me. "How do you know for sure when labor pains start?" she asked. I laughed aloud at that one because that was one question I remember asking my mother when I was expecting Trevor. I was so worried I wouldn't recognize when the labor had started. My mother's answer was simple. "You don't have to worry. Believe me, when the contractions begin, you'll know it." Her answer hadn't satisfied me at the time and it did not satisfy Jessie now either. "I know what pain feels like," she said, "and I know my body. Can't you compare it to a pain I've had before?" she reasoned. But I told her the fact is that labor pains are not like any other pain you've ever had. So I found myself repeating Nana's simple advice; "don't worry, when the contractions begin, you'll definitely know it's time."

It was three o'clock in the morning when she said, "I hope I die before you and dad, 'cause I couldn't bear to be here without you." She had that same look she had when she was a little girl and would run to me all frightened at the first loud clap of thunder, looking to me for reassurance. "When we're in heaven," she wanted to know, "will I know I'm Jessie, and do you think I'll know who you and dad and Trevor are?" It's funny, Hailey, how sometimes when your children ask you a question about God that is impossible to explain in words, He surprises you with just the right way to help them understand. When Jessie asked me what it would be like when we're in heaven, suddenly this story from my own childhood popped into my head and it seemed to be what she needed to hear.

"When I was a little girl," I began, "I remember sitting on the counter while Nana was baking toll house cookies. First, she opened a blue and white can with this creamy white substance inside that looked so delicious I begged to have a taste. Nana told me it was shortening and I wouldn't like it at all. Still, I begged and begged until she finally agreed to let me taste it. And oh, it was awful, not at all like I had imagined. Not a moment went by until she took out this small brown bottle, opened the cover, and let me smell it. It smelled so deliciously sweet that I begged to try that too. 'This is vanilla extract, and even though it smells so good it is very bitter and will burn your tongue," she warned. But I couldn't believe anything that smelled that good could taste that bad, so she put a little bit on the spoon and let me have a taste. She was right. It did burn my tongue, and tasted horrible besides, though I didn't say a word about it and neither did she. Nana was good like that. Next, she took out a bar of deep, dark, chocolate. You'd think I would have learned my lesson by then, but no, I had to taste that too, even though Nana patiently explained that this was bittersweet cooking chocolate, not the kind you eat. Still, I didn't believe her, and for the third time I had a bitter taste in my mouth.

"I hated to admit how many times I had to try things out for myself simply because I wouldn't take my mother's word for it. It took years of lessons, but I finally realized my mother was only trying to save me from having to learn things the hard way. She loved me very much and had no other motive than wanting what was best for me. In time, I was able to trust what she told me without having to have proof!

"Jessie, the whole feeling about dying and going to heaven is like that. There are just some things God couldn't explain to us in words. Think about this. If I can't even accurately explain child birth pains to you when I've gone through it, and like you said, you have a body and have felt pain, then how could we expect God to be able to tell us in words what heaven will be like? How could we possibly comprehend this higher spiritual dimension while we still live on this earth? To help us be able to know God better until we could experience heaven for ourselves, Jesus gave us the picture of God as a loving Father, One who loves us more than we could ever love our own children."

"No, Jessie," I said. "God loves us so much that I'm sure even the plan for death will be something good for us; something that, like labor pains, will bring forth new life. And because of that reason, I am not afraid of it."

Hailey, I will always remember the look of peace your mother had when she smiled at me, assured the final clap of thunder was nothing to be afraid of because she had learned to love and trust both God and me.

Trusting in God, believing, was something Bob certainly did, and there were many people who had helped him along in his journey. One person especially was Stella, a dear friend and the youth minister at his parish. Stella was the one who explained the Christian symbol of the butterfly to Bob, how the butterfly represents and symbolizes the Resurrection. It has three phases during its life: the caterpillar, which just eats, symbolizes normal earthly life. The cocoon resembles the tomb. And the butterfly represents the resurrection into a glorious new life. The butterfly is such a perfect visual for us to understand the metamorphosis, the change that awaits our spiritual evolution. Without our seeing it, the caterpillar's body changes in that seemingly lifeless shell; next comes the necessary struggle to break free – and finally the new 'life form emerges – a creature that is able to fly!

AnneMarie was 17 years old when she died on August 17, 1997. She was going to enter her senior year of high school. Since she died, gardens and butterflies have had a way of turning up for Bob and his family at the most significant times. He even planted a butterfly garden in hopes of stacking the deck in his favor. But the funny thing is, his butterfly garden rarely attracts much in the way of butterflies. He smiles when he says he has a much better chance of finding its resident dragonfly than any more colorful insects.

But some days, he goes on to say, the echo of loss gets a little stronger or more resonant, usually because something will be happening that will be a strong reminder of what is missing. And the funny thing is that, on those darkest days, butterflies would appear. Even in the dead of winter, while typing with a BMT patient online, he'd suddenly realize that his favorite CD had a circle of embossed butterflies in the pattern below the writing. His face softens when he says that he doesn't need butterflies every day, but they sure came in handy the year after AnneMarie's passing.

A Hug

That year the support group was having their reunion in Washington to join the "Cancer March on Washington." They arrived early on Friday to settle in and get together with friends before the actual events started. They met up with the first friend, AnneMarie's runner from Team in Training from a few years back, and headed into the city to grab lunch. (The Leukemia and Lymphoma Society's Team in Training raises money for a cure for blood cancer and makes connections with an honored patient so they know just who and what they're doing it all for!) Coming around the block, leaving all the tall hotels and municipal buildings to the open space of the mall, Bob was greeted by a 3-4 inch Monarch that seemed to be floating on the breeze in front of him saying, hello, it's about time you show up! And that would have been okay, he told us, his weekend would have been made!

The day progressed smoothly as they enjoyed the afternoon with another good friend who is doing okay in his own battle with leukemia, though a very treatable form, Bob admitted. As they crossed the Mall heading to the Lincoln Memorial, they passed the Smithsonian building called "the Castle." In front of it was a sign advertising some event that was coming up soon. Because they were moving and talking, he had time only to notice its title that was "Talk to my Heart." He might have read the rest of it, he said, smiling, if his eyes hadn't been diverted by the appearance of a second butterfly that decided it was time to go by him and head to the rose garden. A second delicately painted butterfly that felt exactly like a hug. Now simply being greeted by two butterflies in this way might seem like a small thing, Hailey, but once God has made a connection with you using a particular sign, it feels exactly like a hug from God when you see it, just like Bob described. While each of these butterflies reached in and touched his heart, when he saw the third butterfly, he described the feeling as letting him know there is a definite plan in God's universe.

One of the things you could do while you were at The March was put up pictures, poems or souvenirs on a Memory Wall. He had brought pictures of both AnneMarie and John Paul. He got there Saturday morning right at 9:00 a.m., and already there were many mementos and notes pinned up. As he finished hanging their square up high in a good place, he suddenly felt the hands of a little boy about five years old tugging on his shirt, telling him to look at what he had put up on the next section of wall. That innocent boy showed him a real butterfly he and his grandmother had found and painted a rainbow over it for his older sister who was eight when she died of cancer. As his mother listened to her son tell Bob about making their square, and how much he missed his sister, she began to weep. Bob was doing his best to console her when a camera crew came up and asked if they could interview the boy. Bob stepped aside and heard that boy's chilling words, "I HATE CANCER!" that said it better than all the speeches made by dignitaries later that day. He said he tried to find the piece the next morning on all the "Good Morning" shows in the area, but finally gave up figuring the little boy had been cut out for a visiting celebrity or two.

The following Easter the family decided to get away for the holiday. A different environment might be a welcomed relief. He could canoe with his son, Andrew, who was 20 months younger than AnneMarie, and take his youngest daughter, Arielle, on a rafting trip on the Lehigh River in the Poconos. After a busy day, when everyone else was asleep, he realized that the holiday and its feeling of something missing had followed him there. As a distraction, he turned on the television. Of all things, HBO was running a special on cancer and he just didn't have the heart to change it. Yet, he kept thinking, "Why am I doing this to myself?"

And just like that, when he didn't expect it, there was the boy with the square he had made with his grandmother, pinned to the Wall with his sister's picture, in her memory. The boy wasn't a sound bite on a morning program but actually part of a great HBO event. "And more than that," he said with tears in his eyes, "I knew he was standing right in front of a picture of the cutest smile that ever graced the planet, and she was reaching out to say…'Dad, gotcha something you'd love for Easter!'"

Five years later, Halloween, would have marked the 5th anniversary of AnneMarie's transplant. The medical community universally accepts the idea that if someone has been cancer free for five years, they are considered cured. That being the case, five years is the accepted traditional celebration time to have had a party. At the party they would have broken their own butterfly snow-globe. Now, Bob decided to break the globe anyway, and sheepishly shared that he expected real butterflies to somehow be flying around. But there weren't any. Going into another holiday season, he was dragging his feet about putting up the decorations and tree. He wasn't wallowing, he assured us, but he was pretty blue.

HBO was running another special called Cancer, Evolution to Revolution. He wondered if that was the Washington March ('98) and figured seeing the boy and the wall again might be just what he needed. Well, he recognized the patient and treatment and watched to see and hear the boy and his words. He knew exactly when they were coming up so he was glued to the set. When they came to the morning of the March there it was, the wall and the boy, and as he waited for him to say his famous three words he suddenly saw himself for the first time standing behind him. Just an average man, of average weight, in average clothes, unnoticeable for his appearance, especially from behind, as he placed a picture of two young people on the Wall of Memory. He looked right at your mother and me when he said, "I don't know why I didn't see myself before, maybe I didn't need to. All I know is that the message was clear to me in the sign that God sent five years later: "AnneMarie and I are still in this together fighting this disease until it's gone."

One thing AnneMarie was very concerned with, and this greatly tugged at Bob and his wife Linda's hearts, was that she wouldn't have a chance to make her mark in life. "What had she been born to do? Was she going to die before she could accomplish it? What was her purpose?" she wanted to know.

Bob was beaming when he told us that AnneMarie had done great things in her short life and had done them proud. AnneMarie was very shy but overcame that shyness to become a spokesperson for the Marrow Donor Program so that others may find a match. To that end, close to a thousand have been tested in her name. Certainly she had a great effect on all her friends who truly appreciated each moment of their lives more for knowing her and, because of their friendship, they never took their own lives for granted. The friends in her close circle were catalysts for change, and Bob was so proud to tell us that all of the girls went on to do some kind of social work. One went on to Yale where she is researching a cure for Crohn's disease. The friends stay in touch with Bob and Linda, which seems to be a miracle in itself for these times. There were weddings to attend and babies to celebrate, and if it couldn't help but remind them that AnneMarie would have been doing all these things just about now, their friendship, loyalty, and love more than made up for it.

AnneMarie's goodness, but also her illness, allowed Bob and his wife, Linda, to experience the real miracles in life; the goodness of the people around her; the countless people who gave blood, who were tested for a transplant. The wonderful, giving soul, as Bob describes the 45-year-old woman from somewhere within two hours of Boston by plane, whose marrow was closer to hers than even her parents' and who agreed to save a girl she'd never known. In marrow so well matched, it starts pumping healthy blood with no blasts (immature blood cells that do not work the way they should). It is important for Bob to tell those who gave so much, that her transplant was a success. That her marrow functioned perfectly and it was fighting the pneumonia with all it had! Unfortunately, it was the lungs that were the problem. They were just too weak from the damage to continue working.

Bob and his family saw other miracles in friends and coworkers who'd show up with food, babysitting or surprises, saying, "You do what you must, we'll do the rest." In other cancer families stopping to build you up even though their own strength and hope could be waning. In the Team in Training runners and walkers who went the distance in your name. In the doctors and nurses dedicating their lives to save hers. "Why try? Why believe?" Bob said, remembering the question he posed to all those who attended AnneMarie's funeral. "I prayed and prayed for a miracle and still I am sitting here in church today. But for those of you crying here saying 'It's true, it's not fair!' I invite you to look around with me and see all the miracles that were part of our journey that brought us here."

At this point he stopped and put his hand to his lips. His eyes are glassy and he jumps to another scene, he remembers another end. It takes a while to say what he wants to say because at this point we are all crying. "As you know," he says, while we are all wiping our eyes, "losing someone is very difficult. Even when they are very sick and you know that they will not be themselves if they 'survive,' it takes an awful lot to say goodbye. Yet, we were able to do that and say, "You're going home, it'll be beautiful. It won't seem long for you until we can get there, you know the way and know we love you." After wiping his eyes several more times before he could continue, he said quietly, "She went peacefully, which was all we had prayed for."

He took a long breath; this had taken a lot out of him. He looked out the sliding glass door, then at us again, and continued. "After she went peacefully, I was able to pack up and go home and even feel calm, which was so different from how I felt for the previous five weeks, or even the previous three years. But I wanted a favor. I wanted AnneMarie to find a way to let me know she was okay and that there really was another side. It isn't easy being good, and I'd hate to go my whole life paying for a ticket just to find out that there isn't a party to get into, if you know what I mean," he said, somehow managing a smile. "Anyway, once we were home we decided we'd wait until 6:00 a.m. to start telling people – let them get a full night's sleep before the ordeal. So we did a few tasks and got ready for the day, but that still left a good hour to try to keep busy.

"I decided to read the Sunday paper which I had seen the delivery person leave in the mailbox. On the way out, I thought of AnneMarie and where she might be. How would I know? I figured it would be in my garden, it was my favorite place and a spot where we often spoke openly and candidly. We had planted a few rose bushes; for sure there would be a beautiful rose there! Checked it out and guess what! No roses. My favorite flowerbed was the one near the mailbox. It would be in full bloom somehow – not too much to ask since it was summer and they were summer perennials. But, five weeks of little to no water and too much heat; they looked mostly dead too.

"I pulled the paper from the mailbox, and was kinda wandering. I had one more hope, another bed next to the garage. You can't see it from the driveway. It was a throwaway bed and there had been a plant I left in there because I wasn't sure whether it was a flower or a weed. I figured, the leafing looked nice enough to be a flower but I wasn't sure, so I never pulled it. Well, here it was. Now four feet tall, topped by a glorious purple flower! Purple was her favorite color!

"I told myself this was my sign. Though, to be honest, does it count if it was here already?" he asked. "Still walking slowly I went into the house mulling over my 'sign' and what I would tell different people on the phone and all the terrible plans I would have to make in the next few hours. I checked the clock; still too soon to wake anyone. I put on the coffee, sat in my big chair and started to read the paper.

"Now," he seemed to confess, "I must say I am a creature of habit, and my Sunday paper is a relaxation ritual. I usually check out the ads, saving a few of the sales and tossing those I don't like, then moving on to the heavy news, the local, the sports, and saving my favorites, the Home Section and Lifebeat, because they deal with fun things that we might try to make our lives a little brighter.

"Still reading and not reading all at the same time, I managed to get through almost the entire paper in less than ten minutes. With only a few sections left, I turned to the next one, which just happened to bear the title HOME. The page was covered with the most gorgeous garden I had ever seen! And it had most of the flowers that are in my own flowerbed. And right in the middle of the garden was a sculpture of an angel. That really touched my heart, but right below it was a wooden sign and in such elegant handwriting was the word: Heaven. In that instant I knew I'd found where AnneMarie was now!" He stopped and put his hand to his lips again.

"She found a way to answer your request," I said softly. "There's no doubt where she is now or that she is definitely okay, and now you'll just have to spend the rest of your life being good! He laughed. "What a fitting sign," I said, "and finding it just where you wouldn't have thought to look."

"That reminds me of one last story I want to tell you," he said. "It's about my wife, Linda, and I know she won't mind my sharing it with you.

"Some people are dog people and some people are cat people. Yes, a few are both, but most have a preference. I am definitely in the first category. Give me something big and cuddly with lots of fur that will adore me forever and I am a happy camper. On the other hand, AnneMarie, who loved her dog, also thought cats were incredible. Their mystiques and disdain for most humanity totally fascinated her, and she wanted one all her life. Thanks to the allergies of her dad and sister that wish pretty much went unfulfilled for most of her life.

"Coming out of her first bout with leukemia she announced that the Perris' cat had kittens, and could she have one." He threw his hand up in the air and smirked. "Yes, she was playing the trump card. And how could I refuse someone who had been through so much? I countered with the allergy card. She gave me that big lip thing and said it would be an outside cat. Well, I don't have to tell you what happened next. Oh yeah, she brought Dandy home a week or two later. She named him Dandy, short for Dandelion, because of the color. He was everything a cat could be and he knew I wasn't his greatest fan and kept trying to butter me up by rubbing my leg. He would meow at her window and be let in. He was all hers, yet, at the same time, he felt he owned the neighborhood. More than one neighbor has felt they were being watched while he lounged on their beds after sneaking in the door when they came home!

"Now, when I got the garden picture sign the day after AnneMarie died, Linda handled it okay, but the truth is she felt a bit left out," he confided. I remember talking about many things that we'd have to deal with, like jealousy, especially thinking of when AnneMarie's friends would be going off to college in a few years, getting married and having children. Talking about our feelings gave us the strength we needed to be able to do the hard things like closing accounts, handling the insurance, paying any bills with her name, and even going out that morning to select the thank-you notes for those who had helped with the service.

"While at the card rack, we each picked a number of cards that were appropriate. We were pretty much finished when Linda spotted a bigger card sticking out from behind one she wanted to read. She picked it up to move it back where it belonged, and in order to do so she had to look at the picture. Lo and behold, it was Dandy, lounging on a daybed with a ton of throw pillows! He would do this in any house he could sneak into. There at the top of the card were the words, 'I was just thinking about you, Mom...' You opened it up and inside it said,' and I wanted you to know I love you.'"

I couldn't help but look over at Jessie. Bob didn't say another word; he couldn't because we were all trying so hard not to cry again.

We sat for a few minutes soaking in the memory of AnneMarie's spirit, thinking of all she had been through in her short life. All the good people who had touched her life, all the lives of the people she had touched, and was still touching. Bob seemed to have said all he had to say.

I was the first to break the silence. "I still have a few questions I'd like to ask," I said. "Ask away," he answered with a wave of his hand. "When you were in the line at John Paul's wake you said to Jackie and Madonna, "welcome to the butterfly club." Is there really an official 'Butterfly Club' that people belong to?" I asked. A big grin crossed his face and he shook his head. There was no such club as far as he knew. "All this time I wondered if the pin you wore on your lapel that day might have been a pin for butterfly club members. But if there is no club," I continued, "where did the pin come from?" He said his friend Stella had given him the pin. It was a gift from the Compassionate Friends, a support group that provides friendship, understanding and hope to those going through the natural grieving process after the death of a child, at any age from any cause. The butterfly is a symbol of hope. They give out butterfly pins and also use the butterfly for their site design," he explained.

"Could we see the pin?" I asked. No pin to be had. Not surprisingly, he had given the pin away to someone in need whose daughter was now fighting cancer. "But who came up with the name, the butterfly club, in the first place?" I asked curiously. "I've never heard anyone else use that term before. It really intrigued me and I've wanted to find out about it since I first heard those words." But he admitted that he never had either, and for some reason he just wouldn't take the credit for it. He insisted that when he welcomed Jackie and Madonna into the butterfly club that day, he had no idea where those words came from.

With that said, our wonderful time together had come to an end. Before we left, Bob entrusted me with what he explained was the first thing he would grab if his house caught on fire – the precious journal one of his friends had made for him and his wife of all the memories of the last five years with AnneMarie. I was honored that he trusted me enough to let me take it with me. As Jessie and I left his house that afternoon, I knew in a small way how AnneMarie's friends felt. I was already more grateful for each moment of my life just having spent one afternoon with her!

Hailey, months have passed since that visit and I've spent every moment I can writing. It's the first day of August and I'm coming to the end of the last chapter of the book. The weather's pleasant as I sit at my desk and enjoy the warm breeze coming in my window. I cannot tell you how alive AnneMarie is, how many times I've read through her journal, how much she continues to affect my life. But after everything has been said and done, I continue to have this feeling inside that there's a piece missing. Where did the butterfly club come from, I keep asking myself? Bob wouldn't take credit for even coming up with the words. I continue to search and pray for an answer.

Bigger Than Life!

It is Saturday. Two weeks have gone by. Two weeks of processing. The butterfly club. Is it a club meant for the many people who have lost loved ones and have experienced butterfly signs from God that have inspired them to go on at the time when they thought they couldn't? Does the sign have to be a butterfly? What about the garden sign that said Heaven? The card with Dandy lounging on a daybed? The fortune cookie, the music, the hat, the Ira card, even the special Santa dog? Those signs were also sent by God to people who have lost loved ones. And what about all the other signs sent by God to comfort, inspire, reassure, motivate, and even hit someone over the head? Would people who have experienced those kinds of signs be included in the butterfly club as well?

I close my eyes for a moment and suddenly AnneMarie's lovely face comes to me from her high school picture I saw in the journal, and it stays with me in the room. This lovely, young girl, 17, so filled with goodness, wondering if she will have time to make her mark in life. Asking, what had she been born to do? Was she going to die before she could accomplish it? What was her purpose?

I leave my desk to sit on the floor on my high back folding cushion chair where I've always been able to reach my deepest thoughts. Suddenly Susan K. Stewart crosses my mind. She went through her own transplant for leukemia in 1989 and was determined to make the path for future transplant patients easier. Her own experience, knowledge, caring and concern for others inspired the founding of BMT Infonet in 1990. BMT Infonet, Blood and Marrow Transplant Information Network, is an InfoNet site dedicated to providing transplant patients, survivors and their loved ones with emotional support and understandable information about undergoing and surviving a transplant. Since its founding BMT has helped transplant patients and survivors worldwide cope with the transplant experience.

My mind drifts to Simon Stephens, the founder of "The Compassionate Friends." As a newly ordained

Assistant Chaplain at the Coventry and Warwickshire Hospital in England, he discovered he was not prepared to deal with the death of a child, yet he was needed to help not just one set of parents, but two. He came to realize that shared experience was the key. When parents lost a child, Simon recognized that the incredible support they gave each other was better than anything he could ever say or provide. Four decades later "The Compassionate Friends" is still connecting grieving parents with other parents who have survived the loss and are learning to live and love again.

I close my eyes again to search through all the bits and pieces and stories Bob shared with us that morning. Just like a game of hide and seek, I find what I had been looking for, as if it has been holding still, patiently waiting to be found. It was hiding in the Candlelight Vigil the Friday evening Bob had gone to the '98 March.

Bob had described it in detail. The night of the Cancer March, many people had been scheduled to speak and perform. Musicians, people in the cancer field, politicians and others were going to tell how cancer had touched their lives. The event was well orchestrated with famous people following lesser known but powerful speakers, and music to keep the evening moving and reaching out to the vast crowd assembled. With the first beat of music of the very first performer, the two huge screens on either side of the stage lit up. On it was the Honor Roll, a list of people who had spent their final days in the battle against this dreaded disease. Every so many seconds another page would come up with about 10 names and a rose beside them. This kept changing and going no matter what was happening on stage. Every five to six pages, a photo would appear. To Bob, seeing AnneMarie's name on the big screen would have meant that he and AnneMarie were still making an impact together.

Bob watched with caught breath for the D's to appear, as he had emailed AnneMarie's name. But the D's came and went and every so often a jumbled list would appear. As they hit the H's Bob was pretty certain that the name he so wanted to see just wasn't going to appear. And he was right; it never did.

Bob had promised to watch for his friend Darlene's daughter's name – Crystal Marie Peterson. He continued his vigil, hoping that in the P's would be a name that would bring joy to someone else who couldn't be there. And as he watched that night, his face must have surely lit up the place like it did when he was talking to us, describing how he was suddenly greeted by the photo of a beautiful face that made the whole night stand still. "There she was, a smile that lights up rooms," he said proudly, "one that was meant to break hearts."

You see, Hailey, Bob's whole life was about doing. He had answered the call to send in pictures knowing the odds they would be used were even less than having a loved one's name included. With all the famous faces, only the smallest percentage of "others" would be shown. And yet, AnneMaire's face was on the big screen reaching out to the vast crowd assembled. He was ecstatic as he summed up his feeling of that unforgettable experience; "I always said that kid was bigger than life, and across the reflecting pool of the Lincoln Memorial, she finally proved it!"

When Bob broke the snow-globe on the 5th anniversary of AnneMarie's passing, the two butterflies *were* finally free, for real, his and her spirits; they were alive in a brand new way. She proved it on the big screen that night. She was there reaching out to the vast crowd; the two butterflies still together, each keeping their commitment to make it better for those still in the battle.

Hailey, in the picture, I finally found what had been missing till that very moment. It was AnneMarie who was the founder of The Butterfly Club! She was the one who had spoken those words through Bob, welcoming Jackie and Madonna as the first two official members. That's why Bob didn't know where the words had come from, and refused to take credit for it. AnnMarie's eternal spirit of goodness was now giving a name to the shared experience of having had a sign from God – The Butterfly Club!

Who would be welcomed into the Club? I suddenly knew it didn't matter if someone had lost a loved one, or if they had been sent a butterfly sign. All that mattered was that God had used a sign to communicate His undeniable presence to them, and they had made the connection. Those welcomed into The Butterfly Club would be able to share their story with others who had felt exactly like they did. They knew!

I sat there for some time. It was like AnneMarie had brought me into her world, the warm and safe world where she was with God. I felt her goodness and understanding of other people's needs. Her great and undying love for her family and friends. I felt her butterfly metamorphosis; the change she had experienced that had brought this new life; the earthly struggle she had gone through that had given her flight! I had no doubt she had made her mark in life and had done what she had been born to do. For the first time in weeks I was completely content; my questions had been answered from above.

Somewhat reluctantly, I got up to leave my writing room, and the calendar on the door caught my eye. In that instant I felt like my heart couldn't hold anymore. It was Saturday, August 17, the day AnneMarie died!

ANNEMARIE DAGESSE
June 4, 1980 – August 17, 1997

EPILOGUE

Hailey, I have shared signs with you, some almost impossible to believe, and yet you have. And to that end, I have one final story to tell you.

A few years ago, on a sky-blue summer's day, I was walking to the house after picking some fresh vegetables from our garden when suddenly I heard these words as clear as a bell; "He-did-it...He-did-it." I stopped walking so I could listen more closely. Sure enough I heard it again, "He-did-it...He-did-it." I called to Grandpa who was in his workshop and asked him to come and listen to what I was hearing. He immediately recognized the song of the black-capped chickadee.

We walked to the edge of the woods where we spotted the pretty little bird nearly hidden on a pine branch, happily calling out his song. I told Grandpa what I had heard, "He-did-it...He-did-it," and asked if he could hear those words too. He listened closely and I could tell he was as amazed as I was. We had both heard the chickadee's call for years and years, but as a background sound, kind of out of focus. We had never actually recognized the words. Hearing them sung so clearly on that picture perfect summer's day seemed like a prayer announcing to the world that God was the One who had created all the beauty that we were seeing. From that moment on, each time the chickadee sang, we heard the words.

Hailey, that experience more than amazed me. A little bird singing the words that now sound as clear as a bell, "He-did-it," was never heard before. It opened my eyes to wonder what else God was communicating that I was missing.

Signs are all around us and when we make the connection there is an immediate feeling of God's presence. The hug from God that Bob felt when he suddenly realized his favorite CD had a circle of embossed butterflies in the pattern. The comfort that permeated Joseph's room the night John Paul's wife saw the 32 butterflies that were in his favorite book for the first time.

God makes Himself known to us in so many ways. He teaches us about life, about our relationship with Him, and about who God is. Through signs like the butterfly we learn that without struggle we will never be able to fly. The black-capped chickadee teaches us the wisdom of a God who is always talking to us, and waits with joy for us to one day make the connection. But how do we learn to recognize the signs?

Though there will always be some people who see and embrace the signs, and others who are in question or never will, perhaps sharing the experience is key, which is one of the reasons I wanted to write this book. Remember when Caleb shared the experience of what butterfly signs meant in other people's lives, his own experience of the butterfly landing on his dad's toe came into his mind? Nancy remembered her butterfly sign only because Jackie and Madonna shared their experience. After Grandpa and I shared our experience of hearing the black-capped chickadee's song, you, Caleb, Ella and Jack heard the words too. And once heard, you can never not hear those words again. Ella named him the "he-did-it" bird.

Hailey, my darling granddaughter, who is growing up too fast; life is full of mysteries. When I was growing up there were some things I could never figure out, like how my mother knew who did it even when she wasn't there to see. When I begged her to tell me how, her answer was always the same, "a little bird told me."

Are the signs just a coincidence, or does God send them? If you want to know for sure, Hailey, the next time you walk near our tall, lovely, pine trees, listen very closely, and I promise a little bird will tell you!

Author Biography

Phyllis Calvey is a writer, speaker, educator, and storyteller with over thirty years of experience in pastoral ministry and religious education. She and her musician/songwriter husband formed The Lighthouse Ministry in 1992 through which they seek to enlighten people in their journey with God by using a presentation format based on stories and songs.

A previously published author with three books and six workbooks to her credit, Calvey currently lives with her husband in Bellingham, Massachusetts, surrounded by her children, grandchildren, and bountiful garden.

Made in the USA
Charleston, SC
04 November 2015